EGYPTIAN·𝓑OOKSHELF

UNWRAPPING A MUMMY

THE LIFE, DEATH AND EMBALMING OF HOREMKENESI

John H. Taylor

University of Texas Press
Austin

International Standard Book Number 0–292–78141–5
Library of Congress Catalog Card Number 95–61446

First University of Texas Press edition, 1996

Designed by Grahame Dudley Associates

Front cover: The mummy of Horemkenesi
after removal of the outer wrappings.

Frontispiece: The team from Bristol City Museum
beginning the process of unwrapping.

Contents

Acknowledgements

The text of this book could not have been written without the help and co-operation of many individuals. Of particular importance have been the specialist reports on the 1981 examination, written by members of the original team of investigators. These reports are the property of the Bristol City Museum and Art Gallery, and have generously been made available to the author in the preparation of the present text. It is to the writers of these reports that most of the observations and conclusions presented in chapters 5–7 should be credited: the late Dr Norman J. Brown (pathology), Professor J. H. Middlemiss (radiology), Dr T. J. Rothwell (blood grouping), Professor J. P. Mitchell (endoscopy), Dr Juliet Rogers and Paul Dieppe (joint and bone pathology), the late F. Filce Leek (palaeodontology and dental report), the late Professor A. I. Darling (dental report), D. P. Dawson (the method of unwrapping and reconstruction of the wrapping procedure), Gillian M. Eastwood (textiles), Dr L. Strong (entomology), Dr D. Gledhill (plant remains), Ernest Pascoe (facial reconstruction), Jonathan H. Musgrave and Suzanne P. Evans (anthropological assessment), Dr A. J. Spencer (decoration of coffin, and inscriptions), Janet Ambers (radiocarbon dating of wood from coffin), J. Lye, N. Hird, S. Bourne and P. Miles (chemical analysis of embalming materials), Mary P. English, M. F. Madelin and R. Campbell (mycological examination of wrappings, and study of facial hair). In addition, the contribution of the following individuals and institutions to the project is gratefully acknowledged: The University of Bristol (in particular, the Medical School and the A. V. Unit), Bristol General Hospital, Bristol Royal Infirmary, Southmead Hospital, Bristol, The British Museum (Department of Egyptian Antiquities and Department of Scientific Research), Dr Joseph Sluglett, Dr Rosalie David, Mike Ponsford, Thea Ovenden, Professor I. R. Harrison and Richard Thorne, Dr Campbell Mackenzie, Professor G. Eglinton, Dr A. E. Jephcott. The radiological survey of the Bristol mummies could not have been achieved without the authority and encouragement of the late Sir Howard Middlemiss, who examined many of the films personally. Preliminary results of more recent studies have been communicated by Dr Robert Miller, to whom grateful thanks are extended. Theya Molleson of the Natural History Museum, London, also provided valuable comments. Valuable assistance throughout the preparation of this book has been received from Sue Giles, Pip Jones, Nicholas Thomas, Jonathan Musgrave, Martin Davies and Dr M. A. Leahy. A particular debt of gratitude is owed to D. P. Dawson for a number of suggestions which have been incorporated into Chapter 5. For any errors, the author alone is responsible. For permission to reproduce the quotation which appears on p. 41, the author is grateful to the University of California Press.

Introduction

On 1 April 1981, a group of scientists gathered around a table in the dissecting room at the University of Bristol's Department of Anatomy. Before them lay the mummified body of a man who had lived in ancient Egypt three thousand years before. The team had assembled to unwrap the mummy and to rescue as much information as possible in the face of the advancing decomposition which threatened to destroy it. Such operations are now undertaken only rarely, for complete mummies with their wrappings intact are far from being an inexhaustible resource. The Bristol unwrapping was embarked upon only after serious consideration, in the light of the body's deteriorating condition, which would otherwise have necessitated its disposal.

The mummy had been found in a rock-cut tomb at Deir el-Bahri on the Theban west bank in 1904–5, enclosed in a painted wooden coffin bearing the name Horemkenesi. A man of this name, who bore the same titles as the owner of the coffin, was mentioned in ancient graffiti carved on the rocks of the Theban necropolis, and it was generally supposed that they were one and the same person. But many questions remained to be answered. Was the mummy really that of the individual in whose coffin it was found? When did Horemkenesi live? How old was he at death? What diseases did he suffer from? What procedures had been used to embalm him? The Bristol team were seeking answers to these, and related, questions, through a combination of historical research and through the unwrapping and dissection of the mummy.

A special table had been constructed, and the team members were armed with a formidable array of dental and medical tools, cameras and recording sheets. Over a two-week period, layer after layer of linen wrappings were carefully peeled away, and each day brought a new discovery: a bandage disclosed an inscription which threw light on the identity of the body; masses of insect remains showed that the mummy had been seriously infested; vital body organs, which the investigators expected to be preserved, proved to be missing. All these pieces of evidence would contribute towards a reconstruction of the individual – his life, his death, his embalming and burial. When the last wrappings had been removed, the researchers saw before them the body of a strongly-built, clean-shaven, middle-aged man; yet they were still at the beginning of their investigations. While study of the coffin-inscriptions and graffiti led to a firm placing of Horemkenesi in a historical and social context, specialist examination of parts of the body built up a picture of his physical attributes and the state of his health. All the body parts were retained for future study. Since the 1981 unwrapping, new methods for the detection of diseases in ancient tissue have added significantly to our reconstruction of Horemkenesi's life, and there can be no doubt that more information will be forthcoming as techniques are developed and perfected. The following chapters summarise what has been learned so far.

The first section of this book examines Horemkenesi's world and uses the surviving records to reconstruct the background against which he lived his life. In the second part the investigation of his body is described, together with the findings, and an attempt is made to create a picture of Horemkenesi as an individual. Inevitably, much must remain conjectural but it is to be hoped that the reconstruction presented here is one which Horemkenesi himself would at least have recognised.

CHAPTER ONE

The Discovery of Horemkenesi

The coffin and mummy of Horemkenesi were discovered late in 1904 or early in 1905 during the excavations at the funerary temple of King Mentuhotep II at Deir el-Bahri. They came to light within the temple enclosure, in the tomb of one of Mentuhotep's wives, which had been reused as a non-royal sepulchre approximately one thousand years after the monument's construction. The site was being excavated on behalf of the Egypt Exploration Fund of London, under the direction of the Swiss archaeologist Edouard Naville, who had already (1893–99) cleared and recorded the temple of Queen Hatshepsut close by. Naville was assisted in the work of excavation by H. R. Hall of the British Museum and the archaeologist Edward Ayrton.

The temple, erected during the middle years of the Eleventh Dynasty (c.2125–1985 BC), lies in an impressive bay of the limestone cliffs on the west bank of the Nile. It faces the modern town of Luxor, the site of ancient Thebes, one of the principal religious and administrative centres of pharaonic Egypt. The existence of the temple of Mentuhotep II had been recognised as early as the 1850s but it was not until Naville's investigations of 1903–7 that the mounds of debris which covered the area were systematically cleared. What came to light was a terraced structure of unique design, combining the royal tomb with a temple for the cult of the deified king and the gods Montu-Re and Amun-Re. Although almost the entire monument was laid bare, initial interpretations of the site's history were confused because of a still imperfect understanding of the history of the Eleventh Dynasty. Subsequent investigations by the Egyptian Expedition of the Metropolitan Museum of Art, New York, and the German Archaeological Institute in Cairo have resulted in a much

1–3 The excavators of the temple of Mentuhotep II: (top) Edward Ayrton (1882–1914); (below left) Édouard Naville (1844–1926); (right) H. R. Hall (1873–1930).

clearer picture of the construction and development of the monument.

The building of King Mentuhotep's temple had occupied many years, during which the design became increasingly elaborate. In its final form it comprised a causeway and a ramp leading to a platform with colonnades on two levels. From the centre of the platform rose a large superstructure, now destroyed, which may have been a pyramid or a replica of the 'primeval mound' (the hill from which, according to Egyptian myth, the sun-god emerged to create the universe). This central feature was surrounded by a columned ambulatory, and behind it stood an open peristyle court which contained the entrance to the king's tomb. Beyond this again, at the base of the cliffs, was a hypostyle hall with a sanctuary for the joint cult of Amun-Re and the king at its western side.

At the rear of the ambulatory were six shrines designed to house the funerary statues of six of Mentuhotep's wives or ladies of the royal harem, named Henhenet, Kemsit, Kawit, Sadeh, Ashait and Mayit. The shrines had been constructed during an early stage in the temple's development, and in a later change of plan they were incorporated into the wall of the ambulatory. Beneath each shrine was a tomb-chamber reached via a pit. These were the burial places

4 *The temple of Mentuhotep II, looking east, during Naville's excavations, 1904–5. The site of Horemkenesi's tomb is at the lower right-hand side of the photograph.*

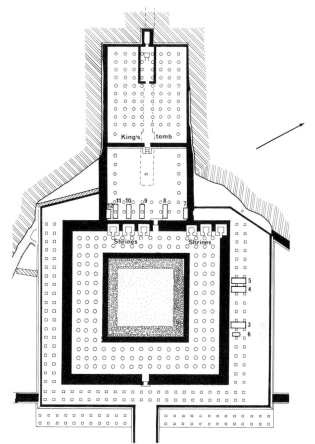

5 *Plan of the temple of Mentuhotep II, showing the location of the tomb shafts behind the shrines of the king's wives. No. 7, the burial place of Horemkenesi, is close to the northern colonnade of the peristyle court.*

of the ladies to whom the shrines were dedicated. The pits, too, had been covered over as plans for the temple grew more ambitious in the later years of Mentuhotep's reign. Columns of the east side of the peristyle court were erected over four of them, while the two northernmost pits were covered by a stone pavement. Four of the burial chambers – those of Henhenet, Kemsit, Kawit and Sadeh – were found in Naville's excavation. All had been plundered, though sarcophagi and other objects (even the mummy of Henhenet) had been left behind by robbers. The other pits, containing the burials of Ashait and Mayit, were found by Herbert Winlock, excavating for the Metropolitan Museum of Art, in 1920–21.

The first clearance of this area of the temple, in Naville's season of 1904–5, was carried out under the supervision of Edward Ayrton. The excavators were in high spirits, for the season had been particularly rich in 'finds', including a series of imposing statues of the Twelfth Dynasty king Senusret III, an exquisite calcite head of a cow, representing the goddess Hathor, and pieces of Eleventh Dynasty relief carving of excellent quality. At the end of 1904 or in the first weeks of 1905 a tomb-pit, subsequently numbered 7, was located behind the third of the shrines from the northern end, that of Sadeh. Descending the vertical shaft, sixteen feet deep and choked with

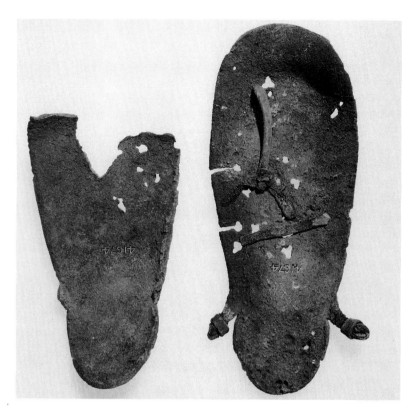

6 *A pair of leather sandals which formed part of the burial equipment of the lady Sadeh, the original occupant of tomb 7. Eleventh Dynasty, c.2050 BC. Max. L. 20.7 cm. EA 41674.*

broken blocks from the temple, Ayrton's men entered the rock-cut burial-chamber. Unlike the other tombs in the series, it contained no sarcophagus – this had perhaps been removed in antiquity. A brief description of the contents of the tomb was published by Ayrton in *The XIth Dynasty Temple at Deir el-Bahari*, I (1907). Lying in the southeast corner were the fragmentary remains of Sadeh's body, together with a 'cartonnage' (probably a mummy-mask) and a pair of leather sandals. At the northern end was the wooden canopic chest containing 'the liver and other viscera', 'packed in a fine black dust.' It was clear that these traces of the original burial had been swept aside to make room for a second occupant, whose painted wooden coffin of mummiform shape lay in the centre of the chamber. This burial was undisturbed and the breast of the coffin was still draped with artificial garlands 'made of plaited rush-leaves threaded on string', which had been placed there by the burial party. The only other funerary goods were some papyrus stalks and 'several sticks with leaves bound to the top' which lay at the side of the coffin. Ayrton assigned the intrusive burial to the Twentieth or Twenty-first Dynasty, probably on the grounds of the style of the coffin. For some reason which was never made clear, he believed the occupant to be a woman. The name on the coffin, initially read in error as 'Hor-siaset (?)', was later correctly interpreted as Horemkenesi.

7 *(Right) Upper part of the coffin lid of Horemkenesi. The head is a standard idealised image of the deceased with the attributes of divinity, including the curled, tapering beard. Above the hands is an image of the sun-god as a ram-headed winged scarab beetle.*

The coffin and mummy were ceded to the Egypt Exploration Fund at the end of the season, as part of the excavators' share of the finds. They were sent to England and exhibited, along with the other major discoveries, at the Society of Biblical Archaeology in London in July 1905. The exhibits were then distributed among the public institutions and private individuals who had subscribed to the excavations. The authorities of the Bristol Museum, a regular sponsor of the EEF's fieldwork since 1884, were keen to obtain some of the finds, and Richard Quick, Superintendent of the Art Gallery and Museum of Antiquities, promptly drew up a list of 'objects desired' from among those seen at the exhibition. The list was rather boldly conceived, for it included, besides the coffin of Horemkenesi, the three black granite statues of Senusret III, the calcite cow-head and numerous pieces of relief carving dating to the reign of Mentuhotep II, which were among the principal finds of the excavators. All of the latter objects were ultimately assigned to the British Museum, but Bristol secured the coffin and mummy of Horemkenesi (and a wooden mallet), which were accessioned in September 1905. What became of the garlands, papyrus stalks and 'sticks' is unknown. The mummy and coffin were registered as Ha 7386 and H 641 respectively, and were displayed in Bristol Museum without attracting particular attention until 1976, when deterioration in the mummy's condition became noticeable. Out of this problem came the proposal to unwrap and dissect the mummy.

A historical 'niche' for Horemkenesi already existed, together with a few clues to his activities in life. The style of his coffin clearly indicated that he had died in the Twenty-first Dynasty (*c.*1069–945 BC), while references to his name in graffiti carved on the rocks in the Theban necropolis – records of official duties – confirmed that he had been active during the early or middle years of the eleventh century BC. The official titles on the coffin and in the graffiti gave a hint of the type of work he did, and provided a clear indication of his rank in the social hierarchy of his time. The body, of course, would provide much more information about Horemkenesi as an individual, but nothing was known of what lay within the wrappings beyond the meagre data obtained from X-rays. It was not even certain that the mummy was really that of Horemkenesi. Ha 7386, therefore, remained a shadowy figure until 1980, when the decision was taken to carry out a full unwrapping.

THE IDENTITY OF HOREMKENESI

Written information about Horemkenesi's identity and the date at which he lived comes from two sources: the texts on his coffin, mummy-board and wrappings; and six graffiti inscribed on the rocks of the Theban necropolis. His name, meaning 'Horus is in the embrace of Isis', seems to have been an uncommon one, and because of its rarity we can assume with reasonable confidence that the Horemkenesi who carved the graffiti was the same man whose body arrived in Bristol three thousand years later.

The texts of the coffin, as is usual, are religious in content, and tell us nothing of Horemkenesi's life, but they are of interest in that they include his official titles:

> Chief of the Gang in the Place of Truth (*Ḥry iswt St-M3ʿt*).
> Great One of the Gang in the Place of Truth (*ʿ3 n iswt n St-M3ʿt*).

These are alternative writings of the well-known title, conventionally translated as 'Chief Workman' or 'Foreman'. 'Place of Truth' was the term commonly used in the New Kingdom (*c.*1550–1069 BC) for the Valley of the Kings, the burial place of many of the pharaohs of the Eighteenth to Twentieth Dynasties. The Chief Workmen, of whom there were two at any one time, were in charge of the craftsmen whose special duty was the construction and decoration of the royal tombs. This community was based in the village of Deir el-Medina on the Theban west bank during the Eighteenth to Twentieth Dynasties, and moved within the temple enclosure of Medinet Habu at the end of that period. The activities, family lives, religious beliefs and judicial system of these workers are very well known from the thousands of records recovered from the village site itself, and from other parts of the Theban necropolis, making Deir el-Medina one of the best-documented communities of ancient Egypt.

> Scribe of the task (?), in the Horizon of Eternity (*Sš ḫn* [? for *sḫn*, 'task'] *m 3ḫt nḥḥ*).

This title, too, associates Horemkenesi with the royal necropolis, for 'Horizon of Eternity' was a common designation of the king's tomb, used interchangeably with 'Place of Truth'. The word *sḫn*, 'task', was occasionally used as a circumlocution for a tomb currently under construction in the royal valley.

> *Wab*-priest in front of Amun in [the temple] 'United with Eternity' (*wʿb* [*n*] *ḥ3t n Imn m ḫnmt nḥḥ*); variant: *Wab*-priest of Amun in 'United with Eternity' (*wʿb n Imn* [*m*] *ḫnmt nḥḥ*).

This title indicates that Horemkenesi was a member of the lower-ranking clergy, and associates him with the image of the god Amun installed in the memorial temple of Ramesses III at Medinet Habu, on the Theban west bank. The inscriptions on the right side of the coffin include a further title beginning with *wʿb*, which may refer to another specific role, but a corruption in the text at this point makes its interpretation uncertain.

> *Wab*-priest of Amun-Re, King of the Gods (*wʿb n Imn-Rʿ nsw-nṯrw*).

The epithet of Amun-Re given here suggests that this title refers to duties within the principal cult-temple of the god at Karnak.

The six graffiti complement the information on the coffin:

The Scribe, Horemkenesi, son of Huysheri (?) (graffito 1012c; on path from Deir el-Medina to Deir el-Bahri).

The *wab*-priest of Amun of Karnak, Horemkenesi (graffito 1313; at the end of the small valley leading to the 'Royal Cache' at Deir el-Bahri).

The *wab*-priest of Amun, Horemkenesi (graffito 1322; at the end of a branch of the Wadi Qubbanet el-Qirud).

The *wab*-priest of Amun, Horemkenesi, son of the *wab*-priest of Amun [in] the [temple] 'United with Eternity', . . . (graffito 1343; at the end of the Wadi Qubbanet el-Qirud).

Year 20, second month of summer, . . . , the coming by the *wab*-priest of Amun-Re, King of the Gods, the Great One of the Gang in the Place of Truth, Horemkenesi, to make initial inspection of the Great Valley, with the agents of the Gang, who were under his direction: Heramunpena(ef), . . . Kenamun and Sapaankh (graffito 2138; Valley of the Kings, east of the entrance to the tomb of Sety II).

The Scribe Horemkenesi . . . The remainder of this text is too damaged to be fully intelligible, but included a mention of the 'Great One of the Gang in the Place of Truth' Nebnefer, and a reference to some official activity in connection with a royal

8 Facsimile of hieratic graffito 1012 carved on the rocks between Deir el-Medina and Deir el-Bahri. The inscription names the necropolis scribes Thutmose and Butehamun, who were active at the beginning of the Twenty-first Dynasty. Horemkenesi has added his name at the right. (After a copy by Wilhelm Spiegelberg).

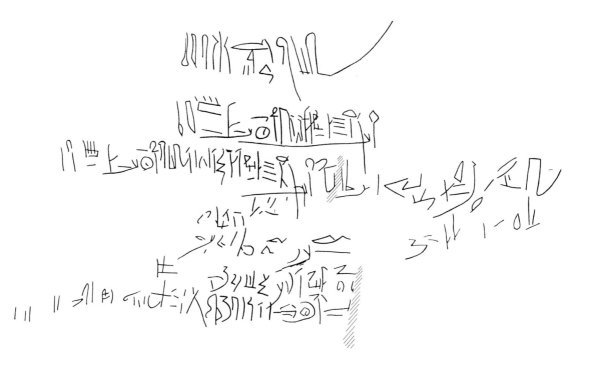

tomb (graffito 3123; Valley of the Queens, end of the left branch of the 'Vallée de la Corde').*

From these texts we learn that Horemkenesi was a scribe, and that his priestly duties involved him in the rituals performed both at Medinet Habu and in the main temple of Amun at Karnak, on the east bank of the Nile. We learn also the name of his father, and the fact that he, like Horemkenesi, had been a minor priest in the temple of Ramesses III.

There are a number of factors which enable the date of Horemkenesi's career to be fixed with probability. Firstly, he is not among the individuals who are known to have held the title of Chief Workman down to the late Twentieth Dynasty. The title itself is not attested after Year 10 of the Twenty-first Dynasty king Siamun (*c*.978–959 BC). Secondly, certain stylistic features of his coffin (the depiction of the hands overlaying the collar; the application of decoration to the interior and the base of the foot) point to a date in the early Twenty-first Dynasty for his burial, as does the method used to embalm him (notably, without subcutaneous packing, which had come into fashion by the time of the High Priest and 'King' Pinedjem I). Thirdly, graffito 1012c is part of a more extensive text, in which Horemkenesi's name is associated with those of the Scribe Thutmose and his son Butehamun. These individuals are well known from many graffiti and other monuments and, above all, from the late Ramesside Letters, a collection of correspondence on papyrus, found at Deir el-Medina in the nineteenth century and now dispersed among various museums. The letters throw much light on events at Thebes at the end of the New Kingdom, and reveal that Thutmose and Butehamun were active in the last years of the Twentieth Dynasty (the 'Renaissance'; see p. 25) and the early Twenty-first Dynasty. Butehamun, in particular, was Scribe of the Tomb under Payankh, Herihor and Pinedjem I, and he is also associated in inscriptions with a Chief Workman Nebnefer – doubtless to be identified with the man of that name mentioned together with Horemkenesi in graffito 3123. Finally, Heramunpenaef, one of the members of the Gang of Workmen who accompanied Horemkenesi on his inspection of the Year 20, is known to have flourished during the last years of King Ramesses XI, when he is several times mentioned in the Late Ramesside Letters. His coffin, now in the Carnegie Museum, Pittsburgh, is of a type characteristic of the early Twenty-first Dynasty.

These factors place Horemkenesi's career within a time-frame bounded by the reign of Ramesses XI (*c*.1098–1069 BC), last pharaoh

---

* Graffito 3898 possibly also named Horemkenesi. The title is 'Great One of the Gang . . .', but the reading of the name is not quite clear: A.-A. Sadek and M. Shimy, *Graffiti de la Montagne Thébaine*, IV/6 (Cairo, 1983), 246.

of the Twentieth Dynasty, and the rule over Upper Egypt of the High Priest of Amun, and 'King', Pinedjem I. The latter's period of office is usually dated c.1070–1032 BC, but recent research suggests that these dates may perhaps be lowered by a few years. The graffito 2138, dated in Year 20 of an unnamed king, has been thought to refer to the reign of Smendes, Ramesses XI's successor in the north of Egypt, but a recent reappraisal of this period suggests that it could relate to the reign of Pinedjem I in Upper Egypt, which for the most part ran concurrently with that of Smendes. Whichever is correct, the date of the event recorded by the graffito probably lies between c.1050 and c.1040 BC. In this graffito, Horemkenesi is already Chief Workman. Since this was the highest-ranking title he bore at the time of his death, it is a reasonable supposition that he did not live many years after making the inspection recorded there. His death may be tentatively placed about 1040–1030 BC.*

* Radiocarbon dating of a sample of wood from Horemkenesi's coffin yielded an age of radiocarbon years 3020 (± 170) BP. After calibration, so that the radiocarbon date can be compared with calendar years, the actual age of the wood could be placed within the range 1450–1005 BC – a figure compatible with the date for Horemkenesi's life based on inscriptional and stylistic evidence.

CHAPTER TWO

Egypt in the Twenty-first Dynasty

oremkenesi lived at a period of fundamental change in Egypt's political organisation, society and economy. By the early years of the eleventh century BC the long and glorious phase of prosperity now known as the New Kingdom (*c*.1550–1069 BC) was coming to an end. During this five-hundred-year period Egypt had risen to become a leading power in the ancient Near East. An active policy of military expansion by the kings of the Eighteenth Dynasty, notably Tuthmosis I and Tuthmosis III, had brought large areas of Syria-Palestine and Nubia under Egyptian control, and by setting up an effective provincial administration the pharaohs were able to exploit the human, mineral and agricultural wealth of both regions. Following a temporary loosening of control during the reigns of Akhenaten and his successors parts of the former Levantine possessions were reclaimed by Sety I and Ramesses II in the Nineteenth Dynasty. Egypt itself was efficiently controlled by a vigorous centralised government, and the economy was healthy. Clear testimony to the wealth and stability of the state in this period were the numerous magnificent temples constructed throughout the land, and particularly at the principal cities of Memphis and Thebes. The latter was embellished with temples at Karnak and Luxor, besides the royal memorial-temples on the west bank, in which the spirits of dead kings received offerings to ensure their survival after death while their mummified and richly caparisoned bodies lay in the rock-cut tombs in the Valley of the Kings.

During the twelfth century BC this magnificent political and economic structure underwent major change. The Mediterranean world was suffering crises which were to leave a permanent mark on its

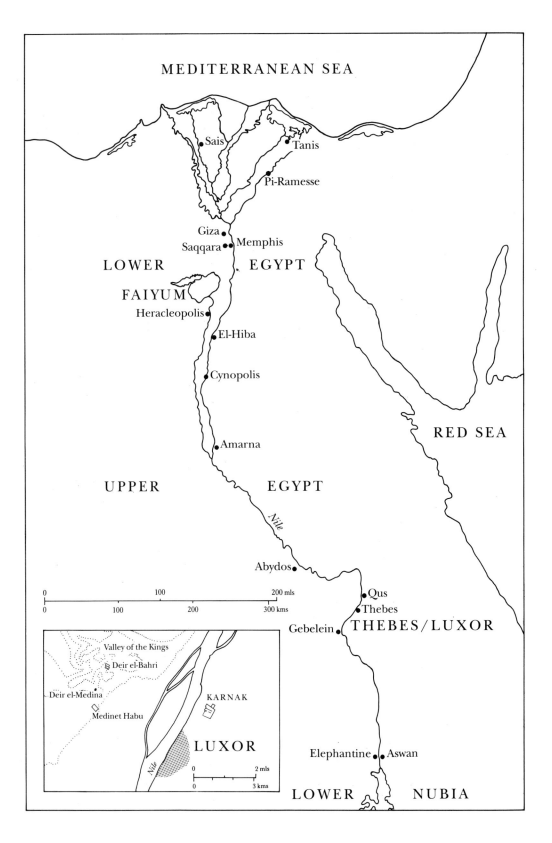

MEDITERRANEAN SEA

Sais

Tanis

Pi-Ramesse

Giza

Saqqara Memphis

LOWER   EGYPT

FAIYUM

Heracleopolis

El-Hiba

Cynopolis

Amarna

UPPER   EGYPT

Nile

RED SEA

Abydos

Qus

Thebes

Gebelein

THEBES / LUXOR

0		100		200 mls
0	100	200	300 kms	

Valley of the Kings

Deir el-Bahri

Deir el-Medina

KARNAK

Medinet Habu

Nile

LUXOR

0		2 mls
0		3 kms

Elephantine   Aswan

LOWER   NUBIA

9 *Egypt in the Twenty-first Dynasty.*

inhabitants and their cultures. The Egyptian king Ramesses III had to fight off repeated attacks by the nomadic Libyan tribes of the western desert and by the Peleset, Tjeker and other groups, now known collectively as the Sea Peoples. These latter, probably from Anatolia and the Aegean, ravaged the eastern Mediterranean. Though the Egyptian state survived (unlike the empire of the less fortunate Hittites in Asia Minor), it proved impossible to exclude permanently the Libyans and other foreign groups who, as immigrants, mercenaries and captives, made Egypt their home and were to have a long-term influence on her history and culture. Egypt lost much of her authority over Syria and Palestine; new states were arising there, and the political power and prestige abroad which Egyptian kings had built up over generations counted for less with the new rulers, who were not prepared to acknowledge the pharaoh as their superior (or even as their equal) merely on the strength of centuries-old tradition. The reassertion of Egypt's old pre-eminence by another phase of military activity such as the Tuthmoside and Ramesside kings had undertaken was now beyond her power. That would have required a strong and efficient administration at home, a stable economy and substantial reserves of wealth and manpower. Far from these being available, Egypt's internal economy was in serious trouble.

Food shortages caused by bad harvests, increases in the price of grain, and rising inflation were symptoms of the economic crisis affecting Egypt during the Twentieth Dynasty. The revenues of the state declined, as the Nubian gold mines became exhausted, and goods and produce from the Levant had to be bargained for instead of simply being demanded as 'tribute'. The cessation of mining operations, for turquoise at Serabit el-Khadim (Sinai) and for copper at Timna (in the Arabah), likewise testify to the contraction of Egypt's foreign contacts. The pharaohs, residing at the city of Pi-Ramesse in the eastern Delta, seem to have become increasingly remote from the administration and events at Thebes, and the situation was probably exacerbated by a rapid turnover of elderly kings after the reign of Ramesses III (*c.*1184–1153 BC). The resulting diminution in the political authority of the ruler had, in turn, a detrimental effect on the administration, which failed to keep the economy running smoothly; already under Ramesses III the royal tomb-builders at Thebes had gone on strike because their 'salary' of food rations was in arrears. The shortage of food led at times to famine; a witness in the trials of Theban tomb robbers under Ramesses XI referred to one recent year as the 'year of the hyenas, when men were hungry'. Embezzlement by corrupt officials went unchecked for years at a time; a revealing picture of official corruption under Ramesses IV and V is presented in the Turin Indictment Papyrus (P Turin 1887), which records (besides numerous other misdemeanours) the theft of over 5700 sacks of

10 *A record of a famine during Horemkenesi's lifetime: the deposition of a witness in the trials of Theban tomb-robbers in the reign of Ramesses XI, mentioning the 'year of the hyenas, when men were hungry'. Papyrus BM EA 10052.*

barley belonging to the temple of Khnum at Elephantine by a ship's captain over a period of about nine years.

More serious were the violent disturbances caused by the presence in Egypt of large organised groups of armed foreigners – chiefly Libyans. This seems to have been an unfortunate consequence of the Twentieth Dynasty pharaohs' policy of settling such groups as troops within Egypt, where some of them acted as garrisons of fortresses, supposedly for the protection of the land. During the reigns of Ramesses III to Ramesses XI, administrative papyri from Thebes mention repeated disruptions involving these foreigners; sometimes they are referred to obliquely as the cause of interruptions in work on the construction of the king's tomb, but there are also more direct references: in the reign of Ramesses VI, some of these 'enemies' destroyed a town, massacring its inhabitants, and putting the authorities at Thebes on the alert in case of an attack. Everyday life and work at Thebes was disturbed, and robbery of royal tombs became serious, as law and order broke down.

The disturbances culminated in a civil war, which seems to have taken place between the seventeenth and nineteenth years of the reign of Ramesses XI (c.1098–1069 BC), when Horemkenesi was probably a young man working at Thebes. Somewhat ironically, the trouble was fomented by an Egyptian – the Viceroy of Nubia, Panehsy, a favoured official who had been installed in Thebes with an army. His task was probably simply to keep order, but the situation seems to have deteriorated. Possibly Panehsy, with troops to provide for in a city already short of supplies, came into conflict with the High Priest of Amun, Amenhotep, whose position gave him control of the vast estates belonging to the temple of Amun. Force was used against Amenhotep, who was deprived of his office for nine months, an event referred to in an inscription at Karnak, and alluded to in Papyrus Mayer A, one of the tomb robbery papyri. Amenhotep appealed to the king for help, and Ramesses XI, perhaps having no other alternative, turned to the general Payankh to defeat Panehsy. In the ensuing conflict, known as the 'War of the High Priest', there was fighting in the north of Egypt, and Panehsy destroyed the town of Cynopolis before he was eventually driven beyond the southern frontier, taking refuge in Nubia. He continued to be a thorn in the side of the administration until the very end of Ramesses XI's reign, when Payankh was still campaigning against him.

General Payankh's defeat of Panehsy's troops left him in charge of one of the major military forces in Egypt. He quickly consolidated his position by taking over all his adversary's offices, including those of army commander and Overseer of Granaries. To these titles he added those of High Priest of Amun and Vizier (chief minister). The holding of military and sacerdotal offices by the same man had been a feature of the Egyptian administration since the Eighteenth Dynasty, and the tendency had developed during the Nineteenth and Twentieth Dynasties, creating a class of 'military-sacerdotal' families who came to wield great influence in the running of Egypt. Payankh's seizure of control, however, marked a turning-point. It was the first time that overall command of the army had been united with supreme religious and executive powers in the person of a single individual, other than the king. Payankh thus became a major power in the land, leaving the pharaoh, Ramesses XI, in a very weak position. Within a short time, a new era, known as the 'Repeating of Births' (or 'Renaissance'), was declared. This was marked by the introduction of a new political arrangement, with Egypt divided into two regions, one comprising the Delta and the Nile valley as far south as el-Hiba; the other consisting of southern Upper Egypt, centred on Thebes. Ramesses XI remained king, but in name only. The northern zone, with its chief cities of Memphis and Tanis, was ruled on behalf of the pharaoh by Smendes, who, though his antecedents are unknown, had probably played an influential role in the recent events. The southern region was controlled from Thebes by Payankh's successors, who combined the offices of general-in-chief and High Priest of Amun. Although the foundation of this Theban line is usually attributed to Herihor, who was army commander and High Priest in the later years of Ramesses XI, a recent re-evaluation of the evidence points to Payankh as the initiator of the new arrangement and the first to hold this exceptionally powerful combination of titles. He was the founder of the military family which held control of the south throughout the Twenty-first Dynasty; they appear to have been of Libyan origin, and may have been descended from some of those groups who had been settled as mercenaries in Egypt during the Twentieth Dynasty.

With the death of Ramesses XI in about 1069 BC, the Twentieth Dynasty and the New Kingdom came to an end, and the division of the country into two principalities was formalised. The term 'Renaissance' was dropped, and Smendes assumed the status of king, ruling from Memphis and Tanis. He and his successors (counted by the historian Manetho as the Twenty-first Dynasty) ruled for about 125 years, but although they were recognised as legitimate pharaohs throughout Egypt, the southern principality, centred on Thebes, continued to function as a virtually independent state under the ruling army commanders. Apparently, an amicable arrangement between the two regimes was concluded, which defined their relative spheres of influence. The Tanite and Theban lines were related by marriage, and it appears likely that the leading figures in both principalities during the first half of the Dynasty were members of one family. Unfortunately, the evidence permits several alternative genealogical reconstructions, so that the circumstances in which the different rulers came to power are still not fully understood.

The bipartition of the country was only one of many changes which mark the Egypt of the Twenty-first Dynasty as very different from that of the New Kingdom. There are in fact strong reasons to regard it as the first phase of the Libyan domination of Egypt (more generally associated with the Twenty-second Dynasty), though historians have been slow to recognise this. Not only do individuals with Libyan names appear in the ruling families in both Upper and Lower Egypt in the Twenty-first Dynasty, but the basic power structure at that time was essentially the same as that which operated during the peak of the Libyan Period (ninth and eighth centuries BC), with power divided between two or more lines of rulers with kingly attributes, and a 'feudalistic' dependence of high officials on local princes. The new regime, however, did not bring renewed prosperity; the decentralisation of Egypt's administration and the continuing weakness of the economy in the Twenty-first Dynasty effectively restricted enterprise at home and abroad. Royal building projects did not equal in scale or magnificence those of the New Kingdom; kings were no longer buried at Thebes, but within the temple enclosure at Tanis, in a completely new type of royal tomb. The costly practice of constructing new tombs for officials was abandoned in favour of the reuse of older sepulchres, or burial in undecorated rock tombs without the conspicuous offering chapels which revealed to robbers the presence of a tomb nearby. Materials of all kinds were recycled – building stone, statues, obelisks, funerary equipment. The frequent 'restoration' and reburial of the mummies of New Kingdom rulers, whose rest had been disturbed or threatened by tomb robbery, provided the authorities at Thebes with an excellent opportunity to relieve them of such gold and precious objects as had escaped the hands of thieves: a source of wealth which helped to boost the unsteady economy. Nubia, meanwhile, seems to have been lost to Egypt (despite the claims of Payankh and Herihor to be viceroys of Kush), and expeditions to the Levant were rare and small-scale events. A papyrus, probably from el-Hiba and now in Moscow, contains one of the most celebrated Egyptian literary texts, the *Tale of Wenamun*, which describes the misfortunes suffered by an official sent by Herihor to the Syrian port of Byblos, to obtain timber for the construction of a state barque for the god Amun. It paints a sorry picture of Egyptian influence in the Levant, for Wenamun's mission becomes fraught with obstacles as the prince of Byblos disputes the authority of the Egyptian rulers, shows scant respect for Amun and refuses to hand over the timber until he receives payment. There is no further evidence for an active Egyptian foreign policy until the reign of Siamun, when Egyptian forces intervened in Palestine against the Philistines. This action was followed by the formation of an alliance between Egypt and Israel, which had been forged into an influential state by David and Solomon. At about this time Solomon took an Egyptian princess (probably a daughter of Siamun) as one of his wives – something unthinkable during the days of Egypt's former glory under the Tuthmoside and Ramesside pharaohs, when Egyptian rulers married the daughters of Near Eastern neighbours but loftily refused to permit the converse. Things had indeed changed.

THE GREAT CITIES: MEMPHIS, TANIS AND THEBES

In the northern principality the two cities of Memphis and Tanis held the most important places. Memphis, situated at the apex of the Delta, south of modern Cairo, was the main administrative centre in the Twenty-first Dynasty. It was a city of venerable antiquity, traditionally the site of the first capital of united Egypt, and lay in the shadow of the great pyramids of the Old Kingdom rulers, standing on the desert edge of Saqqara and Giza. It was from Memphis that Smendes issued a command for repair work to be carried out at Thebes to protect the temple of Luxor from flooding, as recorded on a stela at Dibabia.

Tanis, in the eastern Delta, was a relatively new foundation, and probably first served as a royal residence under Smendes. It possessed an inland port and, strategically located on a branch of the Nile running to the Mediterranean, acted as an important link between Egypt and the Levant, besides commanding the river route used by shipping passing upstream to Memphis and the interior of Egypt. It was in all these respects the successor to the city of Pi-Ramesse, the favoured residence of Ramesses II and the later pharaohs of the New Kingdom, about 20km to the south. By the late Twentieth Dynasty Pi-Ramesse was in decline, perhaps because the Pelusiac branch of the Nile on which it stood was silting up, hampering communications. The kings of the Twenty-first Dynasty remorselessly stripped the city of its large monuments, dismantling them and transferring columns, gateways, obelisks, shrines and colossal statues to Tanis, where they were re-erected or cut up and reshaped to be put to other uses. The aim was to create a fully equipped new metropolis as a northern counterpart to Thebes, with the minimum of labour and expenditure, and this thrifty recycling programme was to create perplexing problems for the modern archaeologists who were faced with the task of reconstructing the

history of the two sites. The main feature of Tanis was the great temple of Amun, standing within a massive enclosure wall, wherein were also other temples and the stone-built tombs of the northern kings. Around these monuments a city grew up, its inhabitants supported by the good agricultural land in the vicinity and the abundant supply of fish and waterbirds.

Control of Upper Egypt during the Twenty-first Dynasty was essentially a military dictatorship, and a string of fortresses was maintained along the Nile. The city of Heracleopolis and the boundary city of el-Hiba were major strongholds (the latter was at some periods a residence of the ruling generals), but the jewel of their state was Thebes, a city which had enjoyed exalted status for a thousand years. It could boast the distinction of having on two occasions produced a line of powerful kings who had rescued Egypt from disunity and weakness, and set her back on the road to prosperity. Its patron deity, Amun, had gradually risen in prominence since the Middle Kingdom. By the New Kingdom he was regularly interpreted as an aspect of Ra, the sun-god. In this compound form Amun-Re, he was the principal deity of the state, and when the riches of imperial exploitation poured into New Kingdom Egypt, Amun's temples at Thebes grew to be the most imposing in the land. By Horemkenesi's time Thebes was no longer a major royal residence but it was the chief administrative base of southern Egypt, and flourished as a religious centre, not least because Amun had now been promoted still further, to become the nominal ruler of Egypt (see p. 32).

The main residential area of Thebes, on the east bank of the Nile, was dominated by the two great temple complexes at Karnak and Luxor. The temple of Karnak, in which Horemkenesi worked, was the chief cult-centre of Amun-Re. On its main axis, running west–east, it was approached from the Nile by an avenue of ram-headed sphinxes, and was fronted by a great pylon gateway, behind which stood the massive columns of the Hypostyle Hall. Beyond this lay further halls, pylons and obelisks leading to the sanctuary containing the cult-image of the god. A temple had existed on the site as early as the Old Kingdom, but most of the structures visible today were erected by the pharaohs of the New Kingdom. On the south side of the main temple was the Sacred Lake in which the priests bathed to ensure their purity in the presence of the god. Alongside this was another processional route leading southwards through a second series of pylons and courts and a further avenue of ram-headed sphinxes. This section of the temple, mainly built during the Eighteenth Dynasty, received special attention during the Twenty-first Dynasty. In this period the Tenth Pylon marked the southern entrance to the temple, and the court beyond it served as the venue for oracular consultations. From this southern gateway ran the processional route to the smaller temple of the goddess Mut, wife of Amun, passing *en route* the temple of Khons, their son. Both these deities were important in the Twenty-first Dynasty, when they were approached, together with Amun, to give oracular pronouncements. The temple of Khons received particular attention under Herihor and Pinedjem I, when the structure was extensively decorated.

The processional way which began at the Tenth Pylon also linked the Karnak complex to 'Southern Opet', now known as the Temple of Luxor. This temple, mainly constructed by Amenhotep III and Ramesses II, was the base of the cult of the divine *ka*, or spirit, of the ruler. At the annual festival of Opet the cult images of Amun, Mut and Khons were transported from Karnak to Luxor temple in their

11 *The first court of the temple of Amun at Karnak. The temple of Ramesses III is in the foreground, with the southern pylons leading towards the Luxor temple in the distance.*

12 Pylon gateway of the temple of the god Khons at Karnak. This well-preserved structure was extensively decorated during the early Twenty-first Dynasty.

portable barques amid scenes of great rejoicing. The festival was the occasion for the magical renewal of the reigning king's *ka* (symbolising his right to rule) through the agency of Amun-Re, and the god himself experienced rejuvenation, thereby ensuring the continuation of the cosmic order.

The houses of the inhabitants of Thebes were clustered tightly around the enclosure walls of the temples. By the Twenty-first Dynasty, houses had even infiltrated the courts of Amun's temple at Karnak; a stela found there records how the High Priest Menkheperre had these houses removed, and erected a substantial wall to the north of the temple to prevent further encroachment.

Crossing the river by boat to the west bank, Horemkenesi would have seen a great plain stretching from the Nile to the wall of limestone cliffs. Behind these cliffs lay a series of valleys and wadis, the burial places of the New Kingdom rulers, dominated by 'the Peak', a mountain whose shape resembled a natural pyramid. Along the foot of the cliffs stood the series of royal memorial temples – each a combination of cult-temple and funerary-temple, in which the dead king was continually reborn through unification with Amun-Re. In the mountain slopes were the tombs of the officials.

The area served as a necropolis as early as the Old Kingdom and continued in use into the Roman period. In the Twenty-first Dynasty, Deir el-Bahri, directly opposite Karnak, was the most favoured area for the burials of the priests and officials of Thebes, probably because of its important religious associations. It was the location of a sanctuary to Hathor, a goddess unequalled in importance in the religious life of the Egyptians. Envisaged as a motherly cow or as an attractive woman, she was both a protectress of the dead and also the promoter of sensuality who gave Amun-Re the erotic stimulus to procreate, thereby ensuring the continuing rejuvenation of the land and its people. Deir el-Bahri was also the focal point of the 'Beautiful Festival of the Valley', a major event in the religious calendar, which took place every year between inundation and harvest. On this occasion the cult-image of Amun-Re crossed the river by barge and was conveyed via a system of canals to the 'Temples of Millions of Years'. The festival culminated in the god's visit to the temples of Deir el-Bahri, where, in the course of his overnight sojourn, took place the rejuvenation of the solar deity on whom depended the fertility of the entire land and the continued existence of the universe. This festival provided the scenario for a reunion of the living and the dead members of Theban families, the funerary images of the dead following that of the god in his procession, after which a rich banquet was held, in which the deceased was 'guest of honour' and the recipient of offerings and prayers to promote his or her transfiguration.

13 Relief in the court of the temple of Khons showing the High Priest of Amun and Army Commander Herihor offering flowers to the Theban god Montu and his consort Tjenenet. Herihor wears kingly regalia and has his names and titles inscribed in cartouches.

Deir el-Bahri was used extensively for burials throughout the

Twenty-first Dynasty. Not only Horemkenesi but most of the leading members of the family of the High Priests of Amun were interred there, often in tombs of earlier periods. It was in one of these family vaults of the High Priests that, at the end of the Twenty-first Dynasty, the remains of many of the pharaohs of the New Kingdom were hidden, surviving untouched until the late Nineteenth Century.

The construction, maintenance and protection of the tombs and memorial temples provided employment for many people, and the West Bank had its permanent residents too. The village of the royal tomb builders nestled in a small valley at Deir el-Medina, hidden from the sight of anyone passing on the river. Administrative buildings were attached to some of the temples, and their enclosures also sheltered the homes of officials.

UPPER EGYPT: THE 'THEOCRATIC STATE' AND ITS EXECUTIVES

The god Amun-Re had already been pre-eminent during the New Kingdom, but in the Twenty-first Dynasty his status rose still higher. Under the ruling generals a 'theocratic state' flourished, based on the concept that Amun-Re, creator of the world, was the supreme ruler of Egypt, his commands being carried out by the High Priest and his subordinates, who acted as the god's deputies. The will of Amun and his 'family', the goddess Mut and the god Khons, was chiefly expressed by means of oracular decrees, and it seems to have been a regular procedure at Thebes for the god's image to be approached directly for an opinion before putting a project into execution (see below, p. 50, for the procedure used in such consultations). While the gods were thus in theory the rulers of the state, the arrangement worked to the benefit of their chief executives, the High Priests, sanctioning with divine authority any plan or appointment they saw fit to make – a particularly useful political tool to consolidate the position of what was effectively a line of foreign rulers. At a more mundane level, the southern rulers' authority was strengthened by their ability to control the still considerable revenues of the Theban temples, and the wealth buried in the necropolis, which they had the opportunity to exploit. It is clear, none the less, that the fundamental basis of their power was military strength; the numerous fortresses which they maintained or built in Upper Egypt are a telling statement of the real character of their rule, and the 'passive' foreign policy of the period perhaps arose in part from a need to direct a substantial proportion of the armed forces towards controlling Egypt itself.

The graffiti carved in the Theban necropolis indicate that it was during the first thirty years of the Twenty-first Dynasty that Horemkenesi was active at Thebes. During much of this period the southern domain was controlled by Pinedjem I, the son of General Payankh. Pinedjem seems to have been the most powerful of the

14 *Colossal statue standing in the first court of the temple of Amun-Re at Karnak. It was originally carved during the reign of Ramesses II and represented that king with his daughter-wife Bint-anath standing before him. The statue was usurped by Pinedjem I in the early Twenty-first Dynasty.*

ruling army commanders, his exceptional influence perhaps deriving both from the inheritance of Payankh's offices and from his marriage to the king's daughter Henuttawy. It appears likely that her father was Ramesses XI, and this link with the old royal line probably helped to gain acceptance for the rule of Pinedjem's family. He had himself depicted wearing royal costume, wrote his name in a cartouche, preceded by the title, 'King of Upper and Lower Egypt', and adopted as his Horus name, 'Strong bull, appearing in Thebes, beloved of Amun'. He was one of the three ruling generals (the others were Herihor and Menkheperre) who adopted kingly titles and were

sometimes depicted wearing royal regalia. Although the exact significance of their 'kingship' is still not fully understood, Pinedjem's use of royal prerogatives was noticeably more ambitious than that of any other Theban ruler of the period, and the principal religious titles were distributed among his immediate family. His daughter Maatkare fulfilled the important post of God's Wife of Amun, while the office of High Priest passed in turn to Pinedjem's sons Masaharta (who died after a relatively short term of office) and Menkheperre. This dominant family even managed to take control in the northern kingdom for, after the death of Smendes and his short-lived successor Amenemnisu, the throne in Tanis passed to another of Pinedjem's sons, Psusennes I. Pinedjem himself perhaps shared honours in the north with Psusennes at the beginning of the new reign – at least, there is evidence that buildings were erected in their joint names. When he died, Pinedjem's body was embalmed and wrapped in a shroud and bandages bearing his names as king, and taken to Thebes for burial.

In his southern domain, Pinedjem I left numerous traces of his activities, though these were for the most part modest in scale. Building works were carried out at el-Hiba and minor restorations and alterations were made to monuments on both sides of the Nile at Thebes. Pinedjem usurped the avenue of sphinxes leading from the quay to the entrance gate (now the Second Pylon) of the temple of Amun at Karnak, and also erected there a colossal statue inscribed with his name. Apart from these routine construction projects the main activity attested in Upper Egypt at this period was the restoration and reburial of the bodies of the New Kingdom pharaohs and their families, several of which had been disturbed by robbers. This long-term programme continued over many years, but there was a heavy concentration of such activity during the time of Pinedjem I. Since this was work in which Horemkenesi may well have been involved, we shall turn next to examine his career in greater detail.

CHAPTER THREE

The Life and Work of a Theban Official

All the surviving references to Horemkenesi's name are from Thebes, and it is likely that most of his life was spent there. As a priest in the temples at Medinet Habu and Karnak he would have worked on both sides of the Nile, but undoubtedly more important were his duties on the west bank, as scribe, and Chief Workman in the royal necropolis. The fulfilling of religious and secular duties by the same individual was characteristic of ancient Egyptian society, in which the service of the gods was performed on a rotational basis by men who were only part-time priests, without a religious 'vocation'. Because of this it should be understood at once that Horemkenesi was not necessarily a devout or spiritual man. His priestly offices were perhaps inherited from his father and would have provided a useful supplement to his income, the bulk of which was probably payment for his duties as an official of the Theban necropolis. Nor would his religious duties have prevented him from marrying and fathering a family, although there is no proof that he actually did so.

CHIEF WORKMAN

Horemkenesi's title of Chief Workman in the 'Place of Truth' associates him with the community of craftsmen who had the special task of constructing and decorating the tombs of the pharaohs in the Valley of the Kings. In the New Kingdom the craftsmen lived near to their work, in a self-contained and closely regulated community at Deir el-Medina. This walled village, occupied from the early Eighteenth Dynasty until the reign of Ramesses XI, was tightly packed with single-storey mud-brick houses and was situated in a small valley

near the Valley of the Kings, which could be reached by means of a path over the hills. The 'gang' of workmen who lived there comprised stonemasons, plasterers, draughtsmen and sculptors. They took their name from the term used to describe the crew of a ship and, like the oarsmen of a Nile vessel, they were organised in two teams, the 'right' and 'left'. Each team was under the control of a Chief Workman, or foreman.

The duties of the Chief Workmen during the Nineteenth and Twentieth Dynasties included controlling the workforce (numbering between 30 and 120 men at different periods) in the day-to-day operations at the king's tomb, overseeing the supply and distribution of tools and raw materials for the workmen's use, and receiving and distributing their wages. Payment was in emmer wheat (for making bread), barley (for making beer), fish, vegetables, water, and wood for fuel. From time to time, cakes, dates, beer and clothing were also provided, and there were bonuses of cooking oil, salt, natron and meat. The Chief Workmen received a higher rate of pay than the ordinary members of the gang; numerous ostraca from Deir el-Medina show that the Chief Workman received 5.5 *khar* of emmer, and 2 *khar* of barley per month, as compared with an ordinary workman's ration of 4 *khar* of emmer and 1.5 of barley (1 *khar* = 76.5 litres). Foremen also acted as intermediaries between the workforce and the senior state officials, the Vizier and the overseer of the Treasury, besides serving as magistrates in the community's local court, and as witnesses to oaths and the sale of property.

15 *Central area of the Valley of the Kings. The entrance to the tomb of Tutankhamun is in the foreground.*

16 *(Above right) Wall-decoration in the tomb of Nefertari, wife of Ramesses II (c.1279–1213 BC), in the Valley of the Queens, one of the finest examples of the work of the Deir el-Medina craftsmen.*

17 *(Right) The village of Deir el-Medina, which housed the workmen who constructed the Theban royal tombs of the New Kingdom.*

At the height of the New Kingdom the appointment of the Chief Workmen was the responsibility of the Vizier (theoretically the king made the appointments, but in practice the Vizier had immediate authority over the craftsmen's community). But the holders of the two posts were understandably reluctant to surrender them and they soon became hereditary privileges of influential families in the village. In the later years of the Twentieth Dynasty the office of foreman of the 'left side' was held by the family of Kaha, that of the 'right side' by the family of Nekhemmut. Unfortunately, information on the holders of the title becomes scanty at the end of the Twentieth Dynasty, so that we do not know whether or not Horemkenesi was in any way related to one of these families. However, as Jaroslav Černy pointed out, a new foreman, if not the son of the previous holder of the post, was normally a member of the community rather than an 'outsider', so it is all the more likely that Horemkenesi's ancestors were inmates of the Deir el-Medina village.

At the end of the Twentieth Dynasty the cutting and decorating of royal tombs at Thebes ceased. The last tomb begun by the craftsmen, that of Ramesses XI, was never finished and never occupied. The civil war and other disturbances of the period made conditions at Thebes unsafe, and in the reign of Ramesses XI the workmen left their village and moved to the relative security of the nearby fortified temple enclosure at Medinet Habu. Shortly after this the gang seems to have disintegrated. Some of the men were conscripted into the army and sent to Nubia to join the general Payankh in his war against the rebel viceroy Panehsy. The conscripts were not only necropolis workers but some of the officials in charge of them, such as the scribe Thutmose. The Late Ramesside Letters reveal that he and his son Butehamun were involved in the obtaining and conveyance of army supplies from Thebes to Nubia. If Horemkenesi belonged to the tomb-builders' community at this time he himself might have been sent to join his colleagues beyond the southern frontier, though there is another possibility. A letter from Thutmose, now in the Berlin Museum, reveals that at the prospect of being sent to the burning deserts of Nubia some of the tomb workers fled to eastern Thebes to lie low.

By the early Twenty-first Dynasty the workmen's community had apparently dwindled to a small residue, headed by the Scribe of the Tomb (the 'secretary' of the gang) and the two Chief Workmen. The necropolis officials were probably occupied largely with the inspection of tombs, the supervision of new burials, and the restoration and reburial of certain mummies which had been disturbed by robbers or were considered vulnerable. Tours of inspection around the necropolis would have formed part of Horemkenesi's routine of work, and it was probably on these occasions that he and his colleagues carved their names on the rocks, where they were found and copied

18 *Letter written by Horemkenesi's colleague, the scribe Butehamun, to the general Payankh. It is written in hieratic script on papyrus, and concerns the carrying out of various commissions. The letter contains a reference to Payankh's ordering the opening of a tomb in the Theban necropolis, probably for the purpose of appropriating its contents. Late Twentieth Dynasty, c.1080–1070 BC. H. 44.5 cm. EA 10375.*

by archaeologists three thousand years later. These 'graffiti' were perhaps intended as a record of the fulfilment of official duties, but it is equally possible that the motivation to inscribe them came from the ancient Egyptians' preoccupation with ensuring that the name (considered to be an essential element in the make-up of the individual) should be preserved for eternity.

The graffiti mentioning Horemkenesi are quite widely scattered, from the Valley of the Kings and the vicinity of the 'Royal Cache' at Deir el-Bahri, to the end of the Wadi Qubbanet el-Qirud, one of the more remote valleys of the necropolis, about 1.7km south-west of Medinet Habu. Such a wide spread of attestations suggests that one of his tasks may have been to search for old tombs. During the Twenty-first Dynasty there seems to have been a general dismantling of the New Kingdom necropolis, involving the emptying of earlier sepulchres, and the confiscation of whatever valuables had escaped the attentions of robbers. It is well known that the royal mummies of the New Kingdom were treated in this way, since texts recording their rewrapping and transfer from tomb to tomb were inscribed in ink on their shrouds and coffins, and have survived to the present day. Among those who are known to have been rewrapped and reburied during the early Twenty-first Dynasty were King Ahmose and his son Prince Siamun, King Amenhotep I and his wife Queen Ahmose-Merytamun, and kings Tuthmosis II, Amenhotep III, Sety I, Ramesses II and Ramesses III. The operations involved removing the

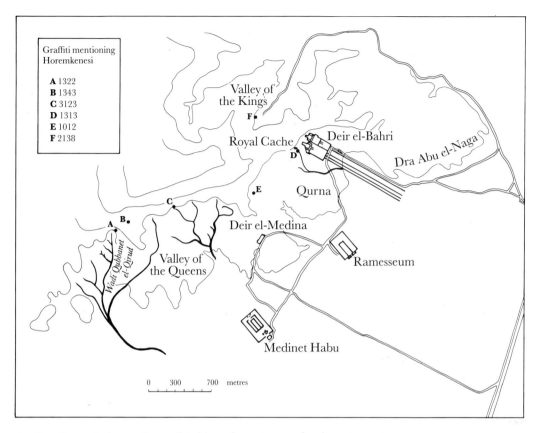

Graffiti mentioning
Horemkenesi

A 1322
B 1343
C 3123
D 1313
E 1012
F 2138

Valley of
the Kings

F

Royal Cache

Deir el-Bahri

Dra Abu el-Naga

D

Qurna

E

C

Deir el-Medina

A B

Wadi Qubbanet el-Qirud

Valley of
the Queens

Ramesseum

Medinet Habu

0   300   700   metres

bodies from their tombs and taking them to a safe place to restore
them – probably Medinet Habu or an unoccupied tomb in the Valley
of the Kings. Here they were rewrapped, often using linen made
originally to clothe the temple-images of the gods. The bodies were
neatly labelled and placed in coffins without gilding or precious
inlays, and most of the valuable items of jewellery which had survived
were removed. This treatment, together with the careful stripping of
gold leaf from their original coffins (where these had survived),
indicates that pious concern for the welfare of the dead was not the
only motivation for the operations. The stresses under which the
economy laboured led the authorities to exploit the wealth buried
with the pharaohs, and the reburials (for which, on at least one
occasion, divine approval was first obtained by an oracular decree)
formed part of an official recycling of valuables. This process continued to the end of the Twenty-first Dynasty and culminated in the
assembling of the two famous caches of royal corpses, one at Deir el-
Bahri, discovered in 1881, the other in the tomb of Amenhotep II in
the Valley of the Kings, which was not found until 1898.

This activity was going on extensively during the reigns of Herihor
and Pinedjem I in Upper Egypt, as is clear from the reburial dockets
inscribed on the mummy-wrappings and coffins, and related texts

19 *(Left) The Theban necropolis, showing the location of graffiti mentioning Horemkenesi.*

20 *The mummy of King Ramesses III, discovered in the 'Royal Cache' at Deir el-Bahri, 1881. On the wrappings is drawn a ram-headed falcon and an ink inscription recording the restoration of the pharaoh's mummy by Butehamun on the orders of Pinedjem I.*

written on the walls of tombs and carved on the rocks in their immediate vicinity. The Chief Workmen were among the small group of officials who were involved in these operations. The necropolis scribe Butehamun, Horemkenesi's colleague, played a leading role, and it is quite possible that Horemkenesi's inspection in the Valley of the Kings in the 'Year 20' was the preliminary to one such operation. Private burials seem to have been treated in the same way, their coffins probably being appropriated for the sake of their gilding and the reusable wood of which they were composed. For a conscientious man it was a depressing prospect, but not all the Chief Workmen known to us were distinguished by their honesty.

SCRIBE

Ancient Egyptian school-texts extol the position of the scribe, praising it above other occupations and stressing its advantages. The following passage from Papyrus Lansing (British Museum EA 9994) is typical:

> *Befriend the scroll, the palette. It pleases more than wine. Writing for him who knows it is better than all other professions. It pleases more than bread and beer, more than clothing and ointment. It is worth more than an inheritance in Egypt, than a tomb in the west.*

(After M. Lichtheim, *Ancient Egyptian Literature*, II, 168)

Since he was a scribe, Horemkenesi must have been fully literate. He would have been able to read and write hieratic, the script of everyday life, as well as some hieroglyphic. He may not necessarily have been fully acquainted with the latter since it was employed chiefly for monumental inscriptions and religious texts, and most of the compositions for which it was used were in Middle Egyptian, a stage of the language which had enjoyed its heyday about 2000 BC. By Horemkenesi's day the spelling, grammar and vocabulary of such texts would have seemed archaic. For day-to-day record-keeping and letter-writing Middle Egyptian had been superseded by a more developed form, now called Late Egyptian. Horemkenesi was perhaps mainly occupied in keeping records of work by his subordinates, inspections of the necropolis, and accounts of equipment and rations supplied for various projects. He would have carried about with him the standard scribe's palette and rush pens. The palette was normally supplied with two cakes of ink, a black one (made from carbon or 'soot') for routine writing, and a red one (made from ochre) for headings and to distinguish significant words or phrases. Notes were made on ostraca (flakes of limestone); more permanent records were written on sheets made from the fibre of the papyrus plant, a costly material and one not to be used wastefully. Palimpsests, documents bearing traces of two or more superimposed texts, show that inscribed papyri were frequently washed clean so that they could be used again.

Of Horemkenesi's childhood and early life we can of course tell nothing with certainty, but what is known of his later career allows us to infer that he had been taught to read and write at this time. Literacy was naturally a prerequisite for obtaining the post of Scribe, and Chief Workmen of Deir el-Medina in the Nineteenth and Twentieth Dynasties seem usually to have been literate. The boys of the necropolis workers' community perhaps obtained their earliest education at the Ramesseum and Medinet Habu temples on the west bank, broadening their knowledge of reading and writing under the guidance of a relative or an experienced elder of the village from whom they could also learn the skills of drawing and painting. But the education of the craftsmen was perhaps not always so informal. A school may also have existed close to the Deir el-Medina settlement, in which boys were taught on a more regular basis. Since succession to an official post was not an automatic consequence of one's rank in society or family connections, a larger number of people were probably educated than eventually held office. Perhaps Horemkenesi showed particular aptitude for reading and writing.

Horemkenesi's command of the written language would have helped him to acquire special status. It has been estimated that under one per cent of the ancient Egyptian population was literate. At its height, however, the community of necropolis workers contained a proportion of literate persons much above the national average – perhaps as high as forty per cent according to a recent estimate.

Medinet Habu: Administrative Centre and Refuge
The headquarters of the Theban necropolis administration in the late New Kingdom was the memorial temple of Ramesses III at Medinet Habu, on the west bank. Completed about eighty years before the accession of Smendes, it was among the most imposing of the series of 'Temples of Millions of Years' which stretched in a line along the plain at the edge of the cultivation. Its central feature was the great temple in which the cult of the dead king was maintained, and the images of Amun, Mut and Khons rested on their annual visit to the west bank at the Beautiful Festival of the Valley. It was fronted by an entrance pylon, beyond which were two courts, three hypostyle halls, various store chambers for temple equipment and offerings, and a whole series of shrines for Amun, Mut, Khons, Ptah-Sokar, Montu, Ra, the deceased Ramesses II, and Ramesses III and his family. On the south side, richly decorated, stood a replica of a royal palace for the use of the dead king's spirit. Most of these features, enclosed within a high wall, were standard elements of royal memorial temples of the New Kingdom. At Medinet Habu, however, the central temple complex was surrounded by two further walls, an outer one of mud brick, faced on the east side with stone and topped at intervals by towers, and an inner one of massive proportions, over

21 *A scribe's palette, with wells for red and black ink, and a central recess for reed pens. Late Period (?).*
H. 32 cm. EA 12779.

22 *Aerial view of Medinet Habu, showing the complex of mud-brick buildings surrounding the temple of Ramesses III. The ruins of the Western High Gate are at bottom centre, and the house of the scribe Butehamun at lower right.*

eighteen metres high and ten to eleven metres thick at the base. This 'Great Girdle Wall' of mud brick probably had a crenellated parapet with small towers. The main entrance to the complex, in the centre of the east face of the Great Girdle Wall, was a massive fortified gate of sandstone and mud brick, fronted by two crenellated towers and linked to the Nile by a canal. A similar gate, now destroyed, stood on the western side.

As the most secure enclosure on the west bank, the 'fortress-temple' was an obvious choice for the base of the administration, and so, while most royal cult-temples fell into disuse soon after the deaths of their founders (their endowments being transferred to other

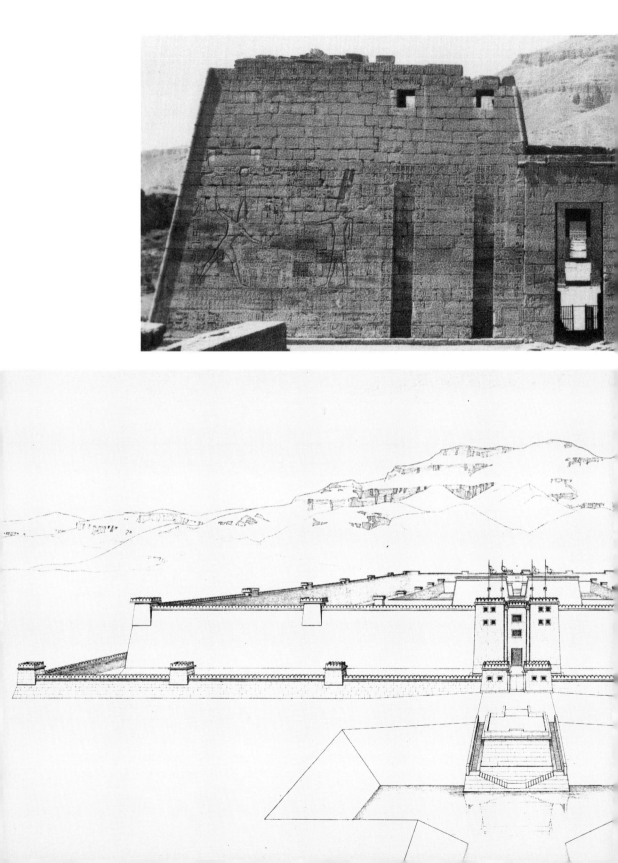

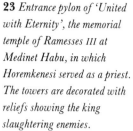

23 *Entrance pylon of 'United with Eternity', the memorial temple of Ramesses III at Medinet Habu, in which Horemkenesi served as a priest. The towers are decorated with reliefs showing the king slaughtering enemies.*

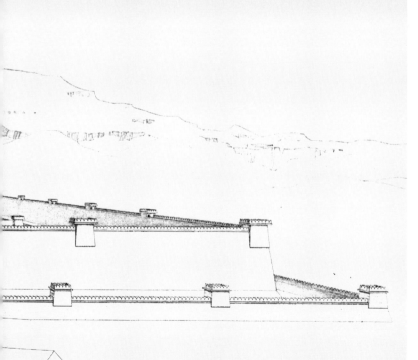

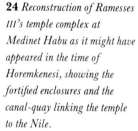

24 *Reconstruction of Ramesses III's temple complex at Medinet Habu as it might have appeared in the time of Horemkenesi, showing the fortified enclosures and the canal-quay linking the temple to the Nile.*

establishments), this one continued to function and develop. It accommodated the offices and houses of officials responsible for running the necropolis and administering the estates which provided the temple's endowments. They would have rubbed shoulders with the military police who maintained order on the west bank, and the priests employed in the temples enclosed by the walls (in addition to Ramesses III's memorial temple, 'United with Eternity', there was a small temple to Amun-Re built by Hatshepsut and Tuthmosis III on a spot considered especially sacred, and known in Horemkenesi's time as 'the holy mound of Djeme'). Medinet Habu also provided a refuge for the inhabitants of the west bank in the face of raids and attacks by bands of marauding Libyans. Even this great fortress was not a guarantee of safety, for during the disturbances at the end of the Twentieth Dynasty the defensive walls were stormed, and the Western High Gate and part of the adjacent Girdle Wall were destroyed (despite the apparent impregnability of the complex, some parts of the structure were relatively easy to capture). The walls were rebuilt by Pinedjem I, though less substantially than before; subsidiary brick

25 *Ruins of the house of the scribe Butehamun, within the enclosure of Medinet Habu. The four surviving palm-columns were originally inscribed with the owner's name and titles, and decorated with religious scenes.*

buildings were renovated at the same time, but the Western High Gate was never repaired.

It was this gate that was used for everyday access to the complex and, in the time of its splendour, Horemkenesi would probably have passed through it on his return after fulfilling some duty in the wadis of the necropolis. Once inside, he would have been confronted by a complex of mud-brick buildings, whose remains were found by archaeologists, filling most of the area between the Girdle Wall and the Inner Enclosure Wall. Just inside the gate, to the right, stood the house and office of his colleague Butehamun, the Scribe of the Necropolis. Its remains were discovered when the site was excavated, with Butehamun's name still legible upon the columns. Walking further, Horemkenesi would see houses, courts, stables, store-rooms and administrative buildings, of mud brick, packed closely together in the confined space. The massive enclosure walls rising up on each side would have dwarfed the low-roofed houses and perhaps created a rather claustrophobic feeling. Though it cannot be identified today, Horemkenesi's own home perhaps stood somewhere in this compound.

Butehamun's house is one of the best preserved at Medinet Habu. Its main room, measuring 5.9 by 5.1 metres, was roughly square, the ceiling supported by four palm-columns coated with stucco and decorated with the owner's name and titles and with religious scenes. In front of this was a smaller transverse room with two columns. A doorway in the rear wall of the main room led to further chambers beyond, which were found destroyed. The roof would have been flat and could have supported a walled garden. The less wealthy Horemkenesi probably lived in a house of similar design, but with less elaborate fittings: the mud-brick walls thinner, and the stone door-frames made of blocks reused from earlier buildings. Several dwellings of this kind were excavated at Medinet Habu, but the names of their owners were not found. Other priests' houses of the Third Intermediate Period, similar in construction to those at Medinet Habu, have been excavated at Karnak between the Sacred Lake and the enclosure wall of the temple of Amun-Re.

HOREMKENESI'S ROLE AS PRIEST

In the ancient Egyptians' conception of the universe, the sun-god Ra held the supreme position as the creator of all life and the agent of resurrection, though creative power was also attributed to other deities such as Ptah, Min, Khnum and Amun. The existence of the universe was believed to depend on a harmonious counterbalance of opposites, embodying both positive and negative forces, and only by constant efforts to perpetuate *Maat* ('Right') could the survival of the cosmic order be guaranteed and the forces of chaos kept in check. In achieving this the temples and the king played crucial roles. The king was the divinely conceived representative of the sun-god on earth, the intermediary between the world of men and the gods. His chief roles were to maintain the cult of the gods and to ensure the supremacy of Right over Wrong. It was in the temples that these all-important activities were focused. The Egyptian temple was not intended as a place where the populace could gather to worship. Its chief function was to preserve the universe in order, and it was in the temples that the carefully balanced relationship between men and gods was perpetuated. At the core of each temple, in the sanctuary, was the 'cult image', a statue of the god, usually made of precious metals, in which the spiritual essence of the divinity was thought to reside. This image had to be bathed, newly clothed and fed every day, in a sequence of ritual acts which also included the reciting of hymns and the burning of incense. Religious festivals, such as the 'Beautiful Festival of the Valley' (p. 31), also played an important part in the perpetuation of *Maat*.

Theoretically the leading role in performing the rituals was fulfilled by the king, but in practice this, and all other duties in the temples, were usually delegated to priests. In the Old and Middle Kingdoms (*c*.2613–1700 BC) temple duties were performed by 'lay priests': local officials and others who served in the temple in rotation, taking time off from their everyday secular tasks. 'Professional' priests, working in the temples full time, do not seem to occur until the New Kingdom. From this date they were very numerous, the higher clergy carrying out the more important tasks of

26 *Wab-priests carrying the barque of the god Montu in procession, depicted in the tomb of Khons at Qurna (Theban Tomb 31). The shrine containing the divine image is partially concealed behind a screen. Nineteenth Dynasty, reign of Ramesses II (c.1279–1213 BC).*

cleansing, clothing and feeding the cult image. For the lesser duties there were still many part-time priests who had secular roles as well. Horemkenesi was just such a person.

The main ranks of the male clergy, in ascending order of importance, were 'pure priests' (wabs, of which Horemkenesi was one), 'god's fathers', and 'god's servants'. The four most senior 'god's servants' were designated as Fourth, Third, Second and First – the First God's Servant being the 'High Priest', the overall head of the temple staff, who also had control of the temple revenues. The office of High Priest of Amun at Thebes was a highly responsible one for, though subordinate to the king, the High Priest enjoyed a large measure of autonomy in his running of the vast temple estates. He might be personally appointed by the king, but the biography inscribed on the statues of Bakenkhons, High Priest under Ramesses II, shows that it was possible for a talented man, rising through the ranks, to reach this post by means of his own ability. Bakenkhons spent four years as a wab priest, twelve as god's father, and fifteen and twelve years respectively as Third and Second God's Servant, before becoming High Priest of Amun. Although the High Priest at Thebes was among the most important figures in Egypt, until the end of the New Kingdom his influence in political and secular matters could not challenge that of the king, because he did not have military power at his disposal. This situation changed dramatically at the end of the New Kingdom, when the generals Payankh and Herihor obtained the post of High Priest of Amun, bringing religious, economic and military authority into the hands of a single person. The adoption of kingly attributes by Herihor, Pinedjem I and Menkheperre may, however, have been chiefly religious in motivation: to fulfil the need for a king as the earthly representative of the creator god, and the champion of Maat, a necessity in a virtually independent state such as that of Upper Egypt.

Information about the actual duties performed by the different grades of priests is incomplete. The 'god's servants' fulfilled the most important roles, deputising for the king in carrying out the daily ritual before the cult image. The lower clergy assisted in these functions, and also performed subsidiary duties. As an ordinary 'pure' priest, Horemkenesi would have been attached to one of the four phyles, or duty-groups, into which the temple priests were divided to serve in rotation. His main task would have been to act as one of the bearers who carried the god's image when it was brought out of the temple-sanctuary in procession at festivals. The cult image was kept in a miniature barque, at the centre of which was a canopy with screens to conceal the god from view. The vessel normally rested in its own chapel in the temple but poles could be attached to the sides so that priests could carry it. A number of depictions, on temple walls, stelae, tomb paintings and ostraca, show the *wab* priests supporting the barque on their shoulders with these poles. Since the images of the gods were normally hidden from sight in the temple sanctuaries, access to which was restricted to the king and the priests, festivals were the only opportunity for the people of Egypt to approach the deity directly.

It was on these occasions particularly that gods might be petitioned to pronounce oracular statements. This was a practice which became widespread during the Twentieth Dynasty, when local gods in towns and villages were often invoked as the highest court of appeal to give judgements in petty arguments over stolen goods and disputed property rights. They might also be sought for more personal reasons: to give protection against disease, to guarantee a good afterlife or to ensure the efficient working of a dead person's *shabti* figures. From accounts of these judgements, it is possible to reconstruct the procedure followed in obtaining an oracular pronouncement. The petitioner stood before the divine image, which was placed in a barque supported on the shoulders of the *wab* priests, and asked for the god's opinion. In many cases, a written question to be answered or a statement requiring approval would be placed before the god, whose acceptance or rejection was apparently indicated by a forward or backward motion of the barque, or perhaps a slight inclination of its prow. The movement resulted from some pressure or force which was supposed to be communicated to the priests who held the carrying poles. The popularity of such consultations towards the end of the New Kingdom may have been due in part to a growing dissatisfaction with corruption in the conventional judicial system, based on the *Qenbet*, or local court. None the less, even the decision of an oracle could be challenged, and Papyrus BM 10335 describes how a man found guilty of theft by an image of Amun at a village on the Theban West Bank took his case to other oracles in the hope of receiving a more satisfactory outcome.

It is difficult to avoid the supposition that kings and high officials manipulated this system for their own benefit. The ruling High Priests of the Twenty-first Dynasty were not slow to see the advantage the process could hold for them. As we have seen, they made use of oracular decrees to sanction their policies; they developed what had begun as a popular practice, carried out in impromptu fashion during a procession, by instituting a regular 'Beautiful Festival of the Divine Audience', lasting for several days, in which the statue of Amun of Karnak, the most prestigious of the divine images of Thebes, was brought forth from his sanctuary specifically to give oracular pronouncements. The solemnity of the occasion was increased by the additional presence of the images of Mut and Khons, and by the staging of the event on the 'Silver Floor of the House of Amun', an especially sacred spot probably located within the court of the Tenth Pylon at Karnak. Records of important oracular judgements were carved on the walls of courts and on the surfaces of pylons along the processional route leading southwards from the sanctuary to the Tenth Pylon.

The necropolis graffiti and the inscriptions on his coffin show that Horemkenesi functioned as a priest in two major temples. He was a *wab* of Amun-Re, King of the Gods, working, as one of the graffiti states, in Karnak, and like his father Huysheri he was also a *wab* of Amun in 'United with Eternity', the temple of Ramesses III at Medinet Habu. This particular form of Amun, like many others worshipped in different temples and chapels, played an important role in local life in western Thebes. Requests for Amun of 'United with Eternity' to be petitioned to give oracular pronouncements survive in letters dating to the very time that Horemkenesi acted as one of the god's attendants, and it is not unreasonable to suppose that he assisted at some of these events.

In one of the inscriptions on his coffin Horemkenesi's title is amplified to *wab en hat*, '*wab*-priest at the front'. In the New Kingdom this title seems sometimes to have connoted a special rank of *wab* priest who walked in front of the god's barque carrying a holy chest, and was entitled to wear silver sandals. But '*wab* at the front' could also be used more generally to identify the group of priests who supported the front ends of the barque's carrying poles. Inscriptions and scenes of the Ramesside period clearly demonstrate this usage, their fellows at the back of the barque being termed '*wab*s at the rear'. This is probably the way in which Horemkenesi's title should be interpreted.

The appointment of individuals to priestly posts was theoretically the right of the king, but in the theocratic state of Upper Egypt in the Twenty-first Dynasty the god himself made or confirmed appointments by oracle. In any case, however, the principle of heredity was a major influencing factor. As the higher priestly posts tended to be, in practice, hereditary possessions passed on from father to son, Horemkenesi's failure to reach higher rank may be a reflection that his ancestors and relatives did not hold more important offices in the temple hierarchy. Perhaps his duties in the necropolis occupied most of his attention and he did not have the opportunity or the desire to further his career as a priest. As the inscription of Bakenkhons, mentioned above, shows, a *wab* priest could attain high rank. An example from Horemkenesi's own time shows that this was still possible: Wennefer of Coptos, who lived under Pinedjem I, records on his stela, now in the Cairo Museum, how he rose from *wab* to become Second God's Servant of Min.

Priestly offices carried stipends which provided a basic 'salary' for the incumbents. Each temple was endowed with land and livestock, which generated 'wages' for the staff in the form of food rations. The

value of individual priestly stipends is unknown, but it was possible to amass offices and thereby create the basis of a sizeable income. These benefits clearly constituted a strong attraction for some to enter the ranks of the priesthood, and records survive of unseemly squabbles over the right to particular revenues. In the absence of coinage, wages in ancient Egypt were paid in kind, chiefly wheat, barley and oil. These items were useful for domestic food production, and doubtless formed the basis of the kind of diet Horemkenesi would have enjoyed. The main food was bread, supplemented with a wide variety of fruit and vegetables, with beer as the staple drink.

Horemkenesi would not, however, always have had to rely on these items to satisfy his hunger. The temple estates also provided the daily food offerings made to the gods. These were prepared in workshops within the temple enclosure, and were consumed by the priests once the god was deemed to have extracted spiritual nourishment from them. Besides bread, beer and wine, the offerings often included meat. This practice sometimes laid bare the human weaknesses of the

27 Figure of Horemkenesi painted on the lid of his coffin. As befits a priest, he is represented shaven-headed, and is dressed in a bag-tunic, linen kilt and decorative collar.

28 *Horemkenesi making an offering to Re-Horakhty, who is accompanied by a winged goddess, probably Hathor; painting from Horemkenesi's coffin lid.*

priests. There were those, apparently, who succumbed to a temptation to 'bypass' the god and to take the consecrated offerings straight to their own tables, to judge from a passage in an address to the priests of the temple of Edfu: 'One lives on the provisions of the gods, but one calls provision that which leaves the altar *after* the Lord has been satisfied!'

When on duty in the temples the Egyptian priest had an obligation to be physically clean. The term for the most basic category of priest, *wab*, means literally 'the pure' or 'purified' and a number of conditions had to be fulfilled in order to ensure this purified state. Herodotus was informed that priests had to bathe in water twice each day and twice at night, and the importance of such libations is amply borne out by texts and depictions of the pharaonic period. The ritual ablutions would be performed in the temple lake, and the water fulfilled a double function – cleansing the body and, symbolically, giving new life to the priest. The head had to be shaved (there were temple barbers whose job was to do this) and, according to

Herodotus, in fact, the entire body was shaved to prevent impurity, particularly the harbouring of lice. Recent studies of the hair of mummies have revealed that these particular parasites were widespread. Priests' clothing, too, had to be of particular materials. Herodotus states that their garments were only of linen, while their sandals were made of papyrus. Wool and leather were not considered suitable. The figures of Horemkenesi painted in the scenes on his coffin probably give a fairly reliable impression of the manner in which he would have dressed. They show him wearing a long 'bag-tunic' of pleated linen covering the upper body and reaching almost to the ankles, with a sash-kilt wrapped around the waist and thighs. His bracelets and ornamental collar would probably be reserved for special occasions.

Horemkenesi would have had to observe certain taboos against eating foods which were considered ritually unclean, notably pig. Fish is also mentioned by Herodotus as a food which priests were required to avoid, and there are clear references to this taboo in texts of the Twenty-fifth Dynasty. Herodotus seems to have been mistaken, however, in stating that beans were also considered ritually unclean.

Horemkenesi would probably also have been required to drink a solution of natron in water for several days preceding a period of duty. Natron, a naturally occurring compound of sodium carbonate and bicarbonate, was extensively used in ancient Egypt as a drying agent in the embalming of corpses. That the drinking of natron was current during the mid-Twentieth Dynasty is known from the Turin Indictment Papyrus (P Turin 1887), a record of accusations made against one Penanqet, *wab*-priest of the temple of Khnum at Elephantine. Among the series of indictments, which cover the reigns of Ramesses III, IV and V, it is stated that Penanqet 'entered with the god' (probably carrying the divine barque) when he had only fulfilled seven of a prescribed ten days of natron drinking. It appears from this that natron was considered to have general purifying qualities apart from its more familiar use as an embalming material.

CHAPTER FOUR

Religious Beliefs
and Funerary
Practices

Long before Horemkenesi's time, surviving death, according to Egyptian belief, was associated with the sun-god Ra and the god Osiris. According to mythology, both of these deities had undergone death and been reborn. The endless cycle of sunset and sunrise was seen as a metaphor for death and resurrection, while Osiris was believed to have been murdered by his brother Seth and subsequently restored to life. These deities, then, extended to all Egyptians the hope of survival beyond death, besides providing a context in which the afterlife could take place. The transfigured dead were envisaged as either accompanying the sun-god as he journeyed through the sky, or as dwelling beneath the earth in the Kingdom of Osiris, harvesting fantastically abundant crops in the 'Field of Rushes'.

During the New Kingdom, progress was made towards a unification of these concepts; religious texts and images in royal and private tombs refer to the idea that Ra and Osiris were temporarily united each night, as the sun-god passed through the terrestrial underworld on his journey to the eastern horizon. By the Twenty-first Dynasty this trend had culminated in the concept of the permanent unity of Ra and Osiris as manifestations of a single Supreme Being who embraced the attributes of all the major gods of Egypt. This 'Great God' travelled across the sky by day and beneath the earth by night, experiencing continual transformations. It was believed that the deceased himself became identified with this being and shared in his transmutation into different forms. The concept of the 'Osirian-solar unity' became very influential and this, alongside the individual solar and Osirian concepts underlay the iconography

29 *A scene painted on the side of Horemkenesi's coffin. The morning sun, depicted as a winged ram-headed scarab beetle, rises from the underworld, represented by the* Djed-*pillar, symbol of Osiris.*

of the richly symbolic images painted on the coffins and funerary papyri of the Twenty-first Dynasty.

Obtaining the desired state of existence after death depended to a large extent on considerations of a more practical nature – preserving the body and keeping the spirit provided with food and drink, while warding off evil influences. The ancient Egyptians believed that every individual possessed spiritual entities, known as the *ka* and the *ba*. For the deceased to survive in the afterlife, the *ka* needed to be nourished and the *ba* periodically reunited with the corpse. The design, decoration and contents of Egyptian graves throughout the entire pharaonic period were directed chiefly towards satisfying these requirements. Mummification was developed in an attempt to preserve the body for eternity. Sustenance for the dead could be provided most simply by placing actual food and drink in the grave, but this could be replaced by an offering cult, and by texts and images which could fulfil the same function by 'magic'. In the New Kingdom, the offering rituals took place in a chapel for the spirit, usually built above or near to the burial chamber and also decorated with appropriate religious texts and scenes.

By Horemkenesi's time the economic weakness of Egypt and the prevalence of tomb-robbing had put an end to the custom of making rock-cut tombs with elaborately decorated cult-chapels. Theban officials were buried in disused tombs of earlier periods (often without decoration), and for the most part without a rich array of burial goods – although this latter phenomenon was perhaps a consequence of a widespread change in funerary customs, rather than a simple indication of limited resources. It has been suggested that the offering cult for the dead may have continued in the Twenty-first Dynasty despite the absence of individual tomb chapels; some central location such as the temple of Hatshepsut at Deir el-Bahri may have served as a communal cult place for the performance of the rituals; another possibility is that cults of the dead continued to be maintained in the houses of their living relatives, a practice well-attested in the New Kingdom. Nonetheless, for the deceased's sustenance and well-being, greater emphasis was now placed on religious texts and images written and painted on coffins and papyrus scrolls, while more attention than ever before was devoted to preserving the body. Indeed, under the sway of the 'theocratic state', there were important innovations in the iconography of funerary equipment, and in the methods used to preserve the corpse.

MUMMIFICATION

By the Twenty-first Dynasty, mummification had been practised regularly in Egypt for at least 1500 years and had reached the peak of its technical sophistication. Written evidence for the methods used by ancient Egyptian embalmers is meagre, and is confined mainly to accounts left by classical authors such as Herodotus and Diodorus Siculus, and a text called the 'Ritual of Embalming'. The latter, known from two hieratic papyri, is of very late date (not before the first century AD) and is concerned mainly with the wrapping of the corpse and the ritual acts that accompanied the operation, although probably reflecting long-established traditions. Fortunately, the procedures used in the Twenty-first Dynasty are well known from studies of many mummies of the period found at Deir el-Bahri in the late nineteenth and early twentieth centuries. In the 'Royal Cache' were the undisturbed bodies of eleven members of the ruling High Priests' families, including those of Horemkenesi's ultimate superiors: Nodjmet, wife of Herihor, Pinedjem I, his wife Henuttawy and their son the High Priest Masaharta. The 'Second Cache' at Deir el-Bahri, discovered in 1891, contained the mummies of 153 of the middle-ranking clergy of Amun, gathered into one tomb at the end of the Twenty-first Dynasty. Many of these mummies were unwrapped and carefully examined by the Australian anatomist Grafton Elliot Smith, who made a comparative study of the procedures used to embalm them. Smith's reports are fundamental sources for an understanding of mummification techniques, and show that the embalmers sought not only to preserve the body tissues, but to restore the corpse as nearly as possible to its appearance in life.

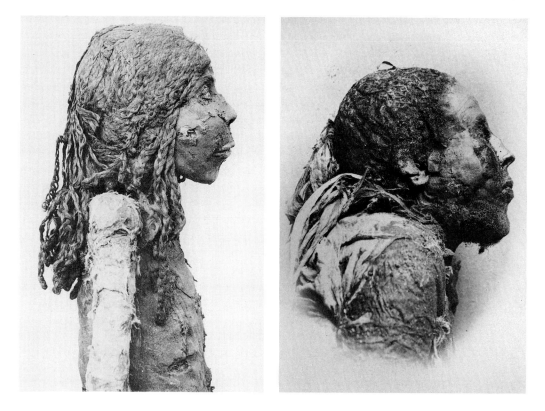

Both ancient Egyptian and classical texts mention seventy days as the usual period between death and burial, during which the embalming took place. The basic steps followed by the embalmers in the Twenty-first Dynasty can be summarised as follows. After a preliminary washing of the body, the internal organs were extracted to prevent them spreading decay throughout the corpse. The brain was the first organ to be removed. Herodotus states that in his time (the fifth century BC) this was done by inserting a hooked metal rod into the nostril(s) and drawing out part of the brain, after which 'drugs' were poured in to extract the remainder. The accuracy of this statement was demonstrated in many of the mummies examined by Elliot Smith. The ethmoid bone, at the top of the nostrils, had been broken, thus creating a free passage to the skull cavity, a phenomenon which has been observed in a few mummies of Middle Kingdom date, and many from the New Kingdom onwards. It is supposed that the bone was broken when the metal hook mentioned by Herodotus was inserted. The function of the brain was not understood by the Egyptians, and for this reason they made no attempt to preserve it. Usually the brain and its associated membranes were completely removed and the cavity was filled with linen cloth and resin, but in some mummies the membrane surrounding the brain and part of the brain itself remained in the skull.

30 and 31 The mummies of two members of the Theban ruling family of the early Twenty-first Dynasty: (left) Nodjmet, wife of Herihor, and (right) Masaharta, son of Pinedjem I. Both were discovered at Deir el-Bahri in 1881. They illustrate the degree of perfection at which the art of embalming had arrived in Egypt by the eleventh century BC.

The next stages involved the removal of the internal organs from the body cavity, and the drying of the corpse. An abdominal incision was made in the left lumbar region, and through this the liver, lungs, spleen, kidneys, stomach and intestines were removed. Care was taken to leave the heart in place, for religious reasons. The drying, which took about forty days, was done using natron, a natural compound of sodium carbonate and sodium bicarbonate, which also contained sodium sulphate and chloride (see p. 54). This substance effectively absorbed all the water in the body, thereby creating an environment unsuitable for the growth of the bacteria which cause decomposition. The natron would probably have been packed tightly inside the body and all around it. Herodotus' account of this process has been variously interpreted, and for many years it was believed that the corpse was immersed in a solution of natron. However, modern attempts to reproduce Egyptian mummification techniques in the laboratory indicate that packing with dry natron crystals is much more efficient than preservation in a liquid natron solution and that after forty days of this treatment the natron could be expected to have absorbed all the moisture in the body. At the end of the drying process the body cavity was probably rinsed to remove any adhering traces of natron; Herodotus and Diodorus mention the use of palm wine for cleansing. This is a plausible method, but archaeology has not confirmed it.

The drying process resulted in the loss of much of the body's subcutaneous tissue, leaving the face and limbs shrunken and distorted. In the Twenty-first Dynasty, string was wound around the finger and toe nails to prevent their loss owing to tissue shrinkage. Besides preventative measures such as this, the embalmers devoted special attention towards making the body appear as natural and lifelike as possible by restoring the fullness of the shrivelled features and limbs. The chief method, attested in many Twenty-first Dynasty mummies, was to stuff mud, linen, sand, sawdust and occasionally other packing materials under the skin of the arms, legs, back, neck and (sometimes in the case of women) breasts. The packing of the legs and neck was done via the flank incision, and involved the embalmer working 'blind' with his hand inside the body cavity. Insertion of packing under the skin of the legs was sometimes done via an incision at the knee, ankle, heel or calf, and further packing was inserted into the foot through an incision between the first and second toes. The back was packed either via the embalming incision or through cuts specially made in the skin of the back. The arms were stuffed via an incision in the shoulder. The face was treated by inserting packing material into the cheeks through the mouth, sometimes using linen, mud or sawdust, and often a fatty substance perhaps containing butter.

The incisions or openings made to pack the body were usually smeared with resinous paste. Sometimes they were covered with pieces of linen or sewn up with string or, in a few cases, patched with leather. Special attention was devoted to making the face appear lifelike. During the embalming, the eyes collapsed into their sockets. They were left in place but artificial eyes made of black and white stone, or of painted linen were inserted, covering the remains of the actual eyes. A thick coating of resin was spread over the face. Partial baldness could be concealed using long strands of plaited hair attached to the head over the real hair.

The viscera which had been removed from the body cavity were preserved in natron and wrapped in linen, much as if they were miniature versions of the body. The liver, lungs, stomach and intestines were each made up into a separate package. From the Old Kingdom to the end of the New Kingdom, and again from the Twenty-fifth Dynasty onwards, these packages were usually placed in sets of four vessels of stone, wood or pottery, now known as canopic jars. In Horemkenesi's time these jars were rarely used, and the visceral packages were usually replaced in the body cavity. Each pack contained, besides its body organ, a wax figure of one of the four Sons of Horus, deities whose role was to extend magical protection over the organs entrusted to them. When the packages had been inserted into the cavity, any remaining space was tightly packed, usually with sawdust, or occasionally with lichen. These substances were probably used because of their pleasant aroma, the sawdust often being made from coniferous wood. The flank incision was normally left gaping and was often covered with a plate of wax or copper alloy; occasionally it was sewn up. A fine gold incision plaque was found on the mummy of Henuttawy, wife of Pinedjem ı. These plaques frequently bear the design of the *wedjat* eye, which – with its symbolic meaning of completeness/wholeness – served magically to heal the wound which the embalmer had been obliged to make.

Finally, the whole surface of the body was painted – red for men, yellow for women – with ochre mixed with gum. This practice is known only from the Twenty-first Dynasty, and seems to have been part of the general effort to make the corpse into a perfect – even idealised – dwelling for the spirit. It may be no coincidence that the colours used in this painting process are those conventionally used in Egyptian art to distinguish men and women, and were so employed in earlier periods on tomb-statues designed to serve as a substitute body for the spirit, should the mummy be destroyed.

The few available accounts of the actual unwrapping of Twenty-first Dynasty mummies suggest that the wrapping of the body proceeded according to a regular pattern, although with numerous variations. The arms were normally extended, with the hands at the sides or outstretched over the pubic region. The limbs were first wrapped individually with bandage-like strips of linen, and were sometimes held in place by twisted strips of cloth. Folded sheets and pads of cloth were added at intervals to help create the standard shape for the body, and one or more layers of powdered vegetable matter (sometimes sawdust) were inserted. In many cases, a thick 'carapace' of resinous paste and linen was applied over the whole body, separating the outer and inner layers of wrapping. Following the application of further bandages, a red-coloured sheet was often wrapped around the body (notably in cases where the painting of the flesh with ochre had been omitted). As the wrapping approached completion, the embalmers put in place a large outer shroud, on which a figure of Osiris was frequently drawn in ink. A series of narrow bandages passing horizontally, vertically and diagonally over the outer shroud completed the wrapping. Within the wrappings of many Twenty-first Dynasty mummies were placed a rolled funerary papyrus, and a selection of amulets for the protection of the deceased, but these were apparently optional.

HOREMKENESI'S COFFIN

In its mummiform shape, with brightly painted religious representations and inscriptions, Horemkenesi's coffin was typical of its period. As usual, a 'mummy-board' (an innermost covering for the body, closely resembling the lid of the coffin in appearance) was provided. However, whereas well-to-do members of Theban society possessed two coffins, nested one inside the other, Horemkenesi had only one. Even that was not made specifically for him; it was a 'ready-made' case, decorated with a standard selection of images and texts, with blank spaces in the inscriptions for the name of the purchaser.

Horemkenesi's coffin was constructed from planks of the sycomore fig (*Ficus sycomorus*), the native Egyptian tree most commonly used for making funerary objects, and was assembled according to a standard procedure well known from other coffins of the period. The flat surface of the lid was made from two pieces of wood, joined end to end, and shaped to represent the contours of the shoulders, elbows and knees. Narrow strips of wood, following the outline of the lid, were attached to the under surface of the main planks, giving the lid a minimum depth of 11–12 centimetres. A large piece of wood slotted between the lower ends of the outer strips served as a footboard on which the coffin could stand upright if required.

The arms, the lappets of the wig, and the slightly prominent abdomen were carved in raised relief from the main plank. To give prominence to the face, arms and upper body, the side walls of the lid gradually increase in depth from foot to head, so that the upper part of the main lid plank projects slightly forward. The coating of plaster which was applied over the whole exterior surface of the lid obscures the finer details of construction, but where this layer has flaked away it is apparent that the shape of the elbows and forearms were created mainly by sculpting the underlying wood. In the area of the abdomen, however, a substantial layer of grey mud plaster is visible, and this was undoubtedly added to help create the fullness of the bodily form. The knees were also represented by slight rounded protrusions. The hands were made from separate pieces of wood pegged to the flat base with dowels, and the face and the front of the wig may also have been made separately and attached in the same way. A small curled beard of wood, imitating the beard worn by Osiris and other deities, was affixed to the chin. The projecting foot is now lost, but well-preserved coffins of similar type show how it would have been constructed, from small pieces of wood attached at an angle to the lower edge of the lid, and extending to the outer rim of the footboard.

A single large piece of timber, adzed smooth, was laid down to form the base on which the mummy would rest. Using axes, adzes and saws with bronze blades, carpenters cut it to the required shape, and filled gaps with small pieces of wood. The sides were formed from two long planks, carefully shaped to reproduce the contours of the shoulders, elbows and knees, and secured to the base with wooden dowels. A curved canopy at the head end and a flat board at the foot completed the outline of the case.

It was the joiner's intention that the lid of the coffin should fit securely to the case by means of a projecting ridge carved from the thickness of the lid, which was supposed to engage in a groove cut into the edge of the case. The work was done very carelessly, however, and a secure fit could not have been obtained by this method alone. As on other coffins of the period, the main method of locking the two halves together was by means of eight wooden tenons projecting from the edge of the lid, four on each side. These fitted into slots excavated in the sides of the case, and were intended to be secured with pegs, hammered laterally through the tenons and through the walls of the coffin as well. It is unlikely that locking pegs were ever used on Horemkenesi's coffin: six of the eight holes into which they were to be inserted are covered by the decoration applied to the exterior of the case. This fragile painted surface would certainly have been damaged during the opening of the coffin had pegs been present.

The mummy-board was constructed simply by hollowing out a single tree-trunk, whose concave section enabled it to fit comfortably over the wrapped body. Small pieces of wood were added to form the sides and top of the wig, the face and the hands. As on the coffin lid, inconsistencies in the outer surface were filled with mud plaster.

Once the work of construction was complete and the surface of the coffin and mummy-board had been given a coating of white plaster to cover blemishes and irregularities, they were ready to be handed over to the scribes and painters who decorated the surfaces. Inspection of the coffin and mummy-board enables the order in which the painting was done to be reconstructed. The exterior decoration of the coffin

32 (Right) Mummy of a Theban priest of Amun, Twenty-first Dynasty, examined by Elliot Smith. The packages containing the embalmed viscera are visible within the chest cavity.

33 (Far right) The case of Horemkenesi's coffin. The internal decoration includes a large composite figure of Osiris, for whose head the upper part of a Djed-pillar has been substituted.

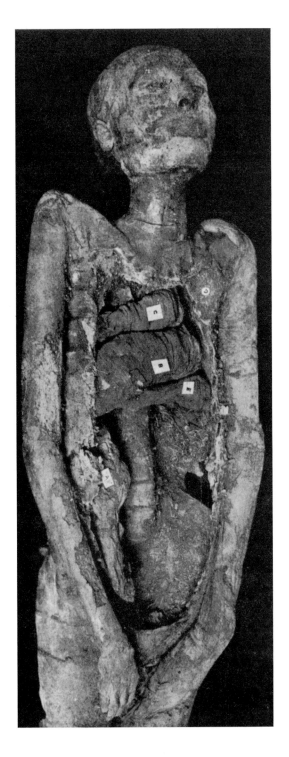

was painted on an ochre-yellow background, that of the mummy-board on a white background. The outlines of all the figures in the scenes, the borders of scenes and texts, details of wig bands, fillet and face were painted in red. Blue, white, green and black were added next, probably in that order (as each colour was added, the craftsman often failed to prevent his paint overrunning what had been applied earlier, a piece of carelessness which has permitted a useful insight into working methods). Blue and green were used for details of the figures in the scenes, for the wig, for the collar, and for elements of the hieroglyphic signs, which had previously been outlined in red. Black and white were used sparingly for small details of the figures, inside and outside. Pink was used for the body of the goddess Nut in a scene on the side of the case (and, curiously, nowhere else). The interior decoration was painted on a dark red ground, with figures in ochre yellow, white, black, dull green and blue. The final stage was the application of the varnish which, by its yellowish hue, helps to give all the coffins of the Twenty-first Dynasty their characteristic appearance. This was applied over the whole of the exterior, except for the wig and the beard. The interior was also unvarnished, with the exception of two uraeus serpents flanking a solar disc at the head end.

Samples of the pigments used on the case of the coffin were studied in the Department of Scientific Research at the British Museum, using the technique of X-ray diffraction (XRD). They were also examined using a binocular microscope and analysed in a scanning electron microscope (SEM), equipped with an energy-dispersive X-ray analyser (EDXA). The following identifications were obtained:

Black	probably carbon black
White	Magnesium calcium carbonate (Huntite)
Red	probably impure red ochre (iron oxide)
Blue	Calcium copper silicate (Egyptian Blue)
Green	probably cuproan-wollastonite
Yellow	Arsenic sulphide (probably orpiment)

The mummiform shape of the coffin emphasises the deceased's association with Osiris, who was regularly depicted in this form. The surface decoration reflects the trends of the period in cramming the maximum potent imagery and textual matter into the smallest available space. One reason for this was that the Twenty-first Dynasty coffin had to accommodate decoration which in earlier times would have been painted on the walls of the tomb-chapel. The exterior of Horemkenesi's case was divided into compartments, filled with scenes which include traditional vignettes from the *Book of the Dead* and subjects used in the New Kingdom, such as the deceased standing before the cow of the goddess Hathor emerging from the western slopes of the necropolis. There were also new images on Twenty-first Dynasty coffins, some emphasising the solar and others

I *and* **II** *The coffin lid (left) and mummy-board (right) of Horemkenesi. Bristol City Museum,* H. *641*

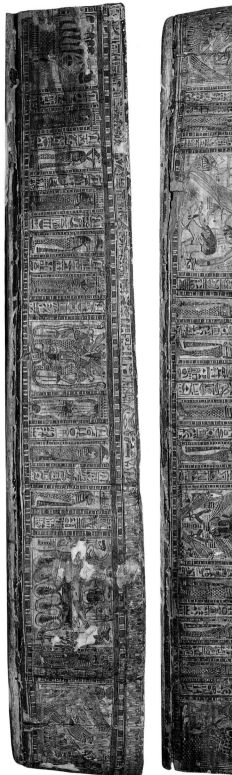

III *and* **IV** *(Left) External surfaces of the coffin case of Horemkenesi, decorated with brief texts and images of resurrection. Bristol City Museum.* H. 641.

V *(Above right) April 1981: the unwrapping of Horemkenesi in progress.*

VI *(Below right) Removal of the filling material from the body cavity.*

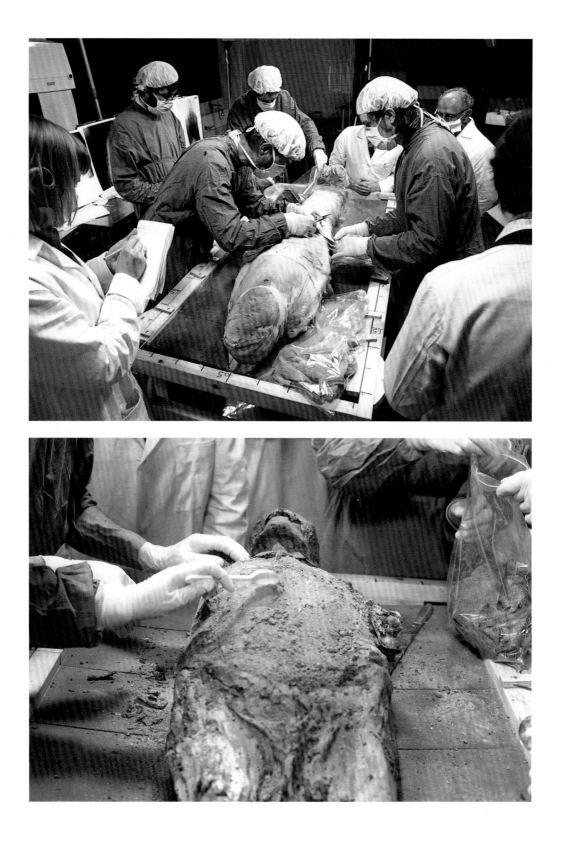

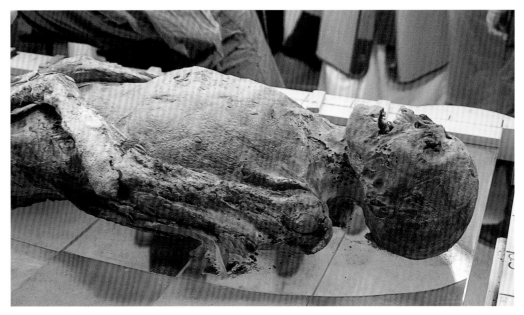

VII *The mummy after removal of the wrappings.*

VIII *Facial reconstruction: the head of Horemkenesi based on a cast of the original skull. The plaster and clay 'half-head' (right) illustrates the technique used to build up the model.*

the Osirian concepts of the afterlife, while some reflect the new idea of the 'solar-Osirian unity' by combining allusions to both concepts within a single image or scene. An example of this is the painting on the side of the case of Horemkenesi's coffin, showing the sun god as a ram-headed winged scarab, above the Djed pillar, a familiar emblem of Osiris. A series of mummiform figures with different heads, painted along the exterior sides of the coffin case, probably represent some of the many forms which the Great God adopted during his transformations (see p. 55). The effort to surround the deceased with as much protective symbolism as possible is seen also in the many tiny signs and figures painted in spaces between the larger scenes, and in the inscriptions – extracts from prayers and formulae, often incomplete, often garbled, a few recognisable words doing duty for the whole text.

The selection and location of the main decorative elements of the coffin were closely linked to the mummy, so that the placing of the mummy inside the coffin was the key which enabled the significance of much of the surface decoration to be clearly understood. The coffin could represent the deceased's universe in miniature. The lid was symbolically the 'sky'; hence an image of the sky-goddess Nut, spreading her wings in protection, was a major feature of its decoration. The case symbolised the netherworld – the region ruled over by Osiris, which was believed to be located beneath the earth. Appropriately, then, an image of Osiris incorporating part of the *Djed* pillar appears in the most prominent position on the interior of the base of Horemkenesi's coffin. The body, occupying the position

34 *Scenes painted on the lid of the coffin: (above) the deceased on a bier re-awakens to new life; (below) the goddess Nut spreads her wings to protect the deceased.*

between these powerful images, was therefore – in a symbolic sense – between heaven and earth, the space in which the sun travels, equating the deceased with the solar deity. Through his position relative to the lid and case of the coffin, he could also assume the role of Shu, god of the atmosphere, who separates heaven and earth in the well-known creation scene of Geb and Nut. And of course he was also identified with Osiris. The deceased was therefore directly linked with the chief deities who were credited with the potential for creation and rebirth. What better way to ensure his own resurrection?

The orientation of most of this symbolic decoration presupposes the mummy to be lying recumbent in its coffin. But during the funeral it was placed upright for the all-important Opening of the Mouth ritual (p. 68). An indication of this is the decoration on the interior of the foot and head of the coffin, which seems to be designed to function with the mummy standing vertically: a Djed pillar beneath the feet again suggesting the earthly region, and a Scarab above the head, the morning sun rising in the sky.

OTHER BURIAL EQUIPMENT

During the seventy days while Horemkenesi's body was in the embalming workshop, other preparations for his burial would be under way. In the early Twenty-first Dynasty a fully equipped

35 *A painting beneath the foot of Horemkenesi's coffin, showing the mummy of the dead man on a lion-bier, attended by the gods Horus and Anubis. Horemkenesi's* ba, *as a human-headed bird, hovers above.*

Theban burial would comprise two decorated anthropoid coffins of wood, a papyrus inscribed with extracts from the *Book of the Dead*, and 401 *shabti* figures to act as the owner's deputies should he be called upon to do any onerous work in the nether world. Canopic containers had become rare because changes in the method of preparing the body had rendered them redundant. Those who had the responsibility of preparing Horemkenesi's funeral were evidently motivated by economy, for they omitted the papyrus and the *shabtis*, and limited expenditure to a single coffin and a mummy-board.

HOREMKENESI'S FUNERAL

The spot chosen for the burial, the temple of Mentuhotep II, was one that Horemkenesi must often have visited in the course of his duties. The king's tomb was still intact as late as the reign of Ramesses IX (*c.*1126–1108 BC), and throughout the New Kingdom the temple acted as a focus for pilgrims who came to make offerings to Hathor. It seems to have been abandoned around the end of the Twentieth Dynasty, perhaps after the site was damaged by a rock-fall. Shortly after this the temple was in ruins and was being used as a quarry. Some of the tombs of the royal women and courtiers which lay within its precincts had been robbed, but they were easily concealed and could be appropriated without difficulty. At least one had been reused at the end of the New Kingdom for the burial of Nakht, a young weaver attached to the temple of King Setnakht whose coffin and mummy were discovered in 1904. Horemkenesi may himself have selected Tomb 7 for his burial, with a view to escaping the attentions of tomb robbers.

At the end of the period allotted for embalming the body, Horemkenesi's mummy, in its coffin, would have been collected by the burial party. For the funeral of a wealthy person a sledge drawn by oxen, or even a wheeled cart, might have been provided, but as Horemkenesi's mourners seem to have spent the bare minimum it is perhaps more likely that a group of men simply carried his coffin to the temple. Unlike the processions of richly laden mourners shown in New Kingdom paintings of the funeral procession, the party which followed was probably empty-handed, with the exception of a man carrying a rolled papyrus, and another with a set of ritual implements and a small stand or table.

At some spot near to the tomb, perhaps in one of the courts of the temple of Hatshepsut close by, the last rites would have been performed. Most important was the Opening of the Mouth ritual, which revivified the body and enabled the spirit to dwell in it again. While one mourner held the coffin upright, a lector-priest read out the words of the ritual from a papyrus-scroll and another mourner took up the ritual implements one by one, from the stand. Incense was burned, water was poured over the coffin, and an offering of the foreleg of a calf may have been presented; all these episodes are shown in depictions of the ritual from the New Kingdom. The most important instruments were an adze, a chisel, a snake-headed rod, and a bifurcate implement called a *pesesh-kef*. With each of these in turn, the officiant touched the eyes, ears, nose and mouth of the face on the coffin, to restore to Horemkenesi the use of his faculties, and enable him to pass into the next world breathing, hearing and seeing.

Meanwhile, other members of the cortège had probably descended the shaft to the tomb chamber. The broken remains of the lady Sadeh, and what remained of her burial equipment, having been swept into a corner, they awaited a shout from above, the signal that the rituals were finished and the coffin was about to be lowered down the shaft. It was manhandled into the chamber and laid down, and the meagre garlands and flowers which had probably been draped over it during the performance of the ritual were placed on the lid and at the side of the coffin. Ascending to the top of the shaft, the mourners found broken paving stones and fragments of the temple masonry conveniently nearby, and these they piled into the shaft before returning to their homes. Three thousand years were to pass before human voices were again heard in that underground chamber, and Horemkenesi was brought forth to begin a journey to a land whose very existence was unknown to the men who had originally laid him to rest.

CHAPTER FIVE

The Unwrapping
and Study of
Horemkenesi

E gyptian mummies have been a perennial subject of interest
since medieval times, when powdered mummy was popularly
used as a medicine. It was only from the end of the eighteenth
century, however, that mummies began to be studied from a more
scientific viewpoint. That was a direct result of Napoleon's Egyptian
expedition and the subsequent deciphering of the hieroglyphic script
which brought about an intensification of interest in ancient Egypt.
During the nineteenth century, many mummies were unwrapped
and examined, often at public lectures. The English surgeon Thomas
Joseph Pettigrew (1791–1865), who 'unrolled' many mummies,
mainly in London, in the 1830s and 1840s was something of a pioneer
in his efforts to obtain scientific data from the bodies. Unlike some of
his contemporaries, who were motivated chiefly by morbid curiosity
and contributed little to an understanding of the past, Pettigrew was
a careful observer and in 1834 published an account of his findings
which is still useful today. The interest created by demonstrations
such as his led to numerous similar events in other towns and cities.
Bristol was the venue for two unwrappings: one in 1824, when the
mummy of the 'Lady Taai' was unwrapped; and a second in 1834 at
the Bristol Institution, the forerunner of the City Museum (Fig. 37).
After 1850, however, the craze for 'unrolling' mummies in public
waned, and while valuable studies were carried out in Egypt, on
mummies unwrapped in the late nineteenth and early twentieth
century, there were fewer investigations in other countries. Since
1900 only four mummies have been unwrapped under controlled
conditions in the British Isles. The last of these was Bristol Ha 7386,
that of Horemkenesi.

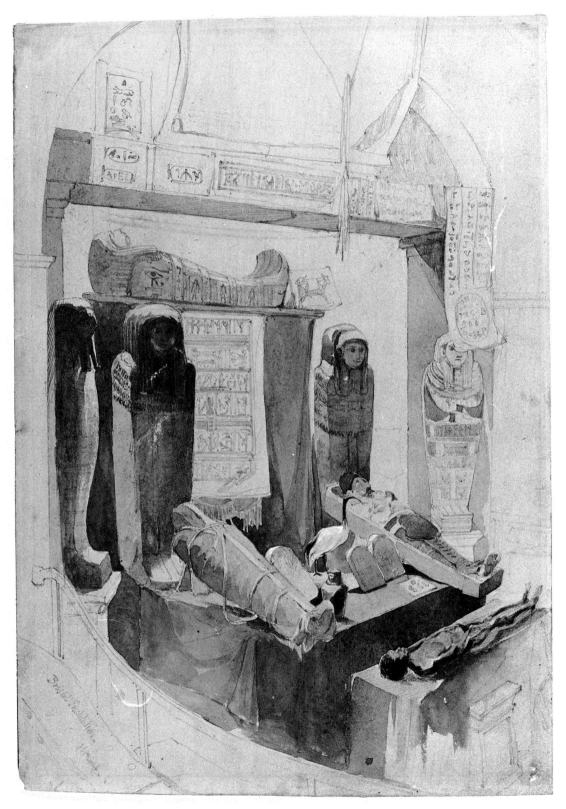

37 *(Left) The theatre of the Bristol Institution in 1834, on the occasion of the unwrapping of a female mummy. The stelae and coffins displayed are now divided between the museums of Bristol and Plymouth. Watercolour by John Skinner Prout (1806–1876).*

38 *(Right) Bones protruding from the decomposing wrappings of Horemkenesi's mummy. The rapid acceleration of this decay after 1976 led to the decision to unwrap and dissect the body.*

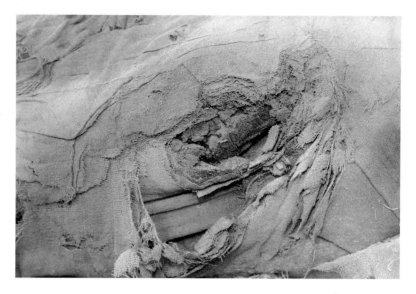

Why was the Mummy of Horemkenesi Unwrapped?

The condition of mummy Ha 7386 had been a cause of concern even before it reached Bristol. Writing in August 1905, Emily Paterson of the Egypt Exploration Fund warned the museum authorities that the mummy they were shortly to receive was in 'bad preservation', adding the ominous note, 'possibly you will have to destroy it.' Nonetheless, the mummy's condition remained stable until just after the unusually hot summer of 1976, when extreme temperatures and consistently high humidity levels were reached in the museum. In the absence of air-conditioning or the means of controlling the temperature and humidity, an encrustation of white alkaline salt appeared on the surface of the wrappings. This proved on analysis to be a sodium compound, originating, it was assumed, in traces of the natron which had been used by the embalmers as a preservative and packing material. It appeared that this substance, perhaps activated by the increased humidity, had begun to migrate outwards and to corrode the linen shrouds and bandages. One elbow became visible where the wrappings were disintegrating and falling away, and as no means of arresting the deterioration could be found, the prospects for the mummy's survival appeared poor. An X-ray examination carried out in 1978 had revealed a number of interesting features which it was thought might repay investigation, and in March 1981, on the initiative of the late Dr Joseph Sluglett, one of the team who had organised and carried out the radiography, the decision was taken to unwrap and dissect the mummy in order to recover as much data as possible. It was hoped that the exercise would establish the individual's sex, age, stature, and other physical characteristics. In particular, the investigators planned to search for signs of any diseases from which the dead man might have suffered, and which might have contributed to his death. A further aim was to discover as much as possible about the techniques which had been used to embalm the corpse. The probability that the mummy was that of a known historical personage lent added interest to the project. Mummies which can be securely identified and dated by reference to monuments or inscriptions other than those from their tombs are surprisingly rare. Thus, the investigators had before them the stimulating prospect that the information recovered during the unwrapping could be placed in a meaningful context.

PRELIMINARIES: RADIOGRAPHY AND TOMOGRAPHY

The modern use of X-rays dates back to 1895. Their value for investigating wrapped mummies was perceived very early, the first X-ray of a mummy being made in 1896 by Walter König, but it was not until the 1960s and 1970s that extensive radiography of mummies in museum collections was accomplished. Peter Gray X-rayed mummies in London, Leyden and Paris, an American team worked on the collection of royal mummies of the New Kingdom in the Cairo Museum, and since then many more radiological studies have been completed. Besides being non-destructive, leaving the body intact for future study, X-rays provide data on age at death, state of health, evidence for disease or injury, and techniques of embalming.

The first glimpse of what lay beneath Horemkenesi's wrappings was provided by the X-rays taken in 1978. These formed part of a radiological survey of all mummies in the Bristol collection, carried out by Thea Ovenden and Joseph Sluglett at the Bristol Medical

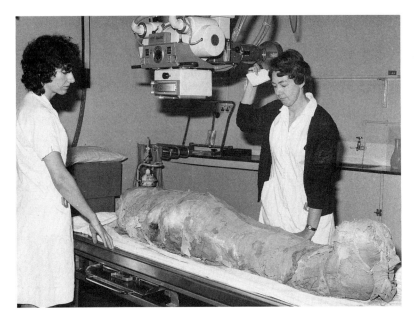

39 *The mummy of Horemkenesi being X-rayed before the unwrapping.*

School. They showed the intact skeleton of a robust man who, on the evidence of the state of his teeth and signs of degenerative changes in his vertebrae, had probably died at about the age of sixty. The arms were seen to have been placed on the front of the body, with the hands over the pubic region. The thoracic and abdominal cavities showed dense opacity, caused by the packing material inserted by the embalmers, and smaller opaque areas appeared between the legs. The X-rays also suggested that there were no amulets, pectoral ornaments or other trappings commonly associated with mummies of the Twenty-first Dynasty. Curiously, the head appeared to be thrown slightly back, with the mouth open.

In February 1981, as a preliminary to the unwrapping, the mummy was X-rayed a second time at Bristol General Hospital. On

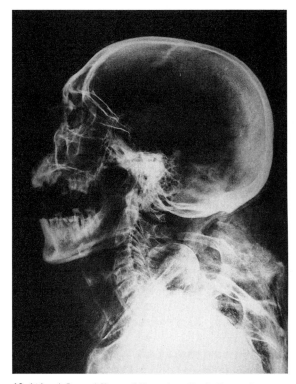

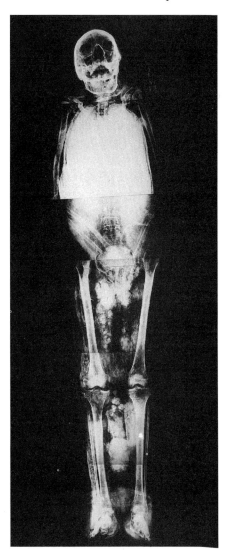

40 *(Above) Lateral X-ray of Horemkenesi's skull, revealing the open mouth.*

41 *(Right) Frontal X-ray of the mummy of Horemkenesi. The dense opacity in the chest cavity is caused by the packing material inserted by the embalmers.*

this occasion it was also subjected to tomography in order to try to obtain clearer images of the densely packed interior of the body, which showed up as opaque areas on the X-rays. The results showed the spine and the outline of the packing material which had been inserted into the abdominal cavity. The team of investigators hoped that within this dense, apparently homogeneous, packing the dead man's internal organs might be found, which would be of prime importance as a potential source of evidence for disease.

Planning the Operation

Since the turn of the century the unwrapping of Egyptian mummies had become such a rare event that no standard procedure could be said to exist, and the many unwrappings carried out in the nineteenth century offered little guidance. Most had been rapid and unscientific operations (King Ramesses II had been divested of his bandages in Cairo in 1886 in less than fifteen minutes), and the final report – if any were published – usually concentrated on what had been found, rather than on the method used to unwrap the body. Of the unwrappings carried out in Britain since 1900, only one could serve in any way as a model for the Bristol team. This study, organised by Dr Rosalie David in 1975, involved the unwrapping of the mummy of a young girl of the Roman period in the Manchester Museum. It broke new ground in bringing together the combined expertise of specialists from many fields, each of whom contributed their scientific knowledge to the study of a different aspect of the project. The techniques applied included radiology, histology, microscopy, chemical analysis, botany and textile studies. The Manchester investigation produced a wealth of information not only about the age and appearance of the dead woman and the methods used to embalm her, but also about her state of health and the environment in which she had lived.

Many of the methods of the Manchester team were adopted for the unwrapping of Horemkenesi: under the direction of David Dawson, Curator in Archaeology and History at the Bristol City Museum, a team of experts from many disciplines was assembled from the Museum, Bristol University Medical School and other establishments, including the British Museum. These included archaeologists, a pathologist, an anatomist, dentist, radiographer, textile expert, entomologist and chemist. The investigations were to follow a logical sequence, beginning with non-destructive methods such as radiography and proceeding with the unwrapping and an external examination of the body. As the corpse was dissected, an internal inspection of all major parts was to be made, using modern scientific techniques of microbiology, histology, endoscopy and electron microscopy, with studies of the wrappings, and of remains of insects and plants, which previous investigations suggested might well come to light. Rosalie David acted as adviser to the team. The actual unwrapping was done by Dawson himself and archaeologist Mike Ponsford, the dissection being undertaken by pathologist Norman Brown and anatomist Jonathan Musgrave. Many samples of hard and soft tissues were kept for study by specialists.

Since the aim was to recover as much information as possible, the work was organised as if it were an archaeological rescue-dig on a miniature scale. Special care was taken to ensure proper recording of the findings, and in particular of the pattern of bandaging – an aspect

42 *Members of the unwrapping team assembled before the removal of the first wrappings. In the centre is Joseph Sluglett (in a dark suit) and, to his left, David Dawson, Curator in Archaeology and History.*

43 *(Below) As the work progressed, a detailed record of the pattern of bandaging was made. The mummy of Horemkenesi lies on the table specially designed to facilitate unwrapping and recording.*

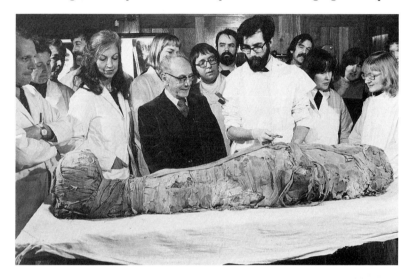

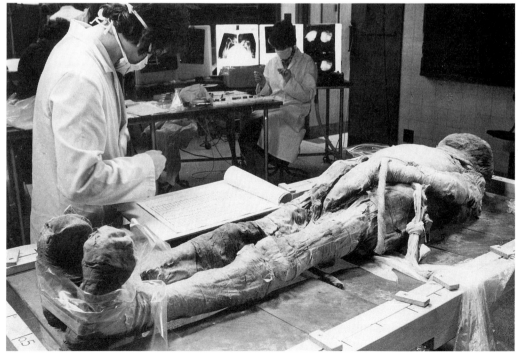

which had rarely been recorded in previous unwrappings. Devising appropriate equipment required some originality. A special table was used, comprising a wooden frame marked with a numbered grid to facilitate recording, and eight moveable trapdoors to allow the team to work both above and beneath the mummy in order to unwind the wrappings without moving the body. Surgical and dental instruments were used to lift and separate the layers of cloth and to take samples of tissue, bone and resin. Each sample taken was placed in a polythene bag and labelled to identify its location. Photographs were taken and drawings made at every stage in the process.

THE UNWRAPPING

The unwrapping took place in the dissecting room at the Department of Anatomy of the University of Bristol, and lasted two weeks. Team members wore protective clothing and face masks to guard against the ill-effects of inhaling dust. The operation was transmitted via closed-circuit television to the entrance hall of the City Museum, in which members of the public could watch every stage in the proceedings on projection screens. The plan to dissect a human body under the gaze of the public inevitably raised questions of ethics and propriety, even though the corpse was three thousand years old and could have no identifiable living relatives. After enquiries to confirm the legality of the arrangements, the investigators decided to proceed, in view of the interest which the unwrapping promised to arouse. Particular care was taken to treat the remains with due respect. Indeed, knowing Horemkenesi's identity helped the team to relate to their subject as an individual and to keep the human dimension of the project constantly in mind. In the event, the televising of the operation proved extremely popular, and no objections were raised.

The first wrappings were removed on 1 April 1981. The mummy, laid on its back on the special table, presented a ragged appearance. The large outer shroud, which covered it from head to foot, was much rotted and holed – even exposing the elbow on the right side – and the outer binding strips which helped to hold the shroud in place were damaged and disordered. These retaining bandages, a standard feature of the wrappings of mummies in the Twenty-first Dynasty, comprised a vertical strip from head to foot, five to eight transverse bands and a diagonal band passing over each shoulder and crossing on the breast. Besides helping to secure the outer shroud they probably also had a religious function. The 'Ritual of Embalming' which, though of later date, may enshrine traditions dating back to Horemkenesi's time, describes the outer wrappings and bindings in terms of a warrior's garments, fitting him for the struggles in the next world, in which he was to 'clear the way before Osiris'.

The single large sheet which these bands retained had been laid

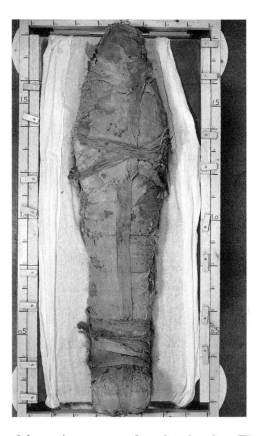

44 The mummy at the beginning of the operation, showing the damaged outer shroud and the disordered binding tapes.

over the top of the entire mummy from head to feet. The edges had been tucked in underneath, where they had been glued into the excess resin that had soaked through the bandages. Once removed, work began on following the outer wrappings. These consisted of strips of linen between 100mm and 160mm wide and up to 2m to 3m long. They had been wound around the body, usually starting at the feet and working up to the chest and shoulders. The ends were not fastened, but simply overlain by the first wind of the next strip. The third day of work provided a welcome surprise; for on one of the bandages was a clear inscription in black ink giving part of the name Horemkenesi. This discovery at once answered one of the team's main questions since it demonstrated that the body they were shortly to disclose really was that of the man for whom the coffin had been made. There is frequently some uncertainty as to whether a particular mummy is actually that of the person in whose coffin it lies. Mistakes were sometimes made by the ancient Egyptians, and coffins were often usurped for reuse – particularly in the Twenty-first Dynasty. As the operation proceeded, a pattern was revealed. Layers of wound strips alternated with layers of sheets placed on top of the body from chin to feet. This thickening of the layers to fill the angle between the feet and the body was augmented by laying scraps of

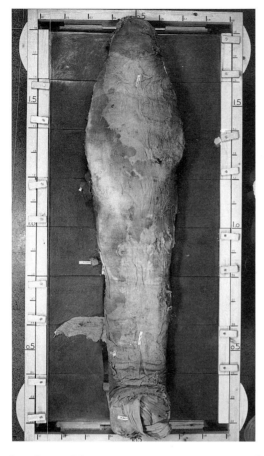

45 *(Left) The wrappings revealed after the removal of the outer shroud.*

46 *(Below) A scrap of bandage bearing the name of Horemkenesi inscribed in ink, found amoung the first wrappings to be removed.*

bandage without any apparent care on top of the sheets. These scraps varied from coarse, worn pieces to torn fragments of finely finished fringe. One of these provided a second inscription in black ink. Part of it had been torn away. Beneath the fourth layer of strips which bound the mummy from chin to feet was a sheet of which the top, covering the face, had been exposed since the first sheet had been removed. It had been wrapped around the head, and the ends gathered together by the chin and twisted to produce a shape resembling that of the divine beard worn by Osiris.

Among the wrappings the team also found fragments of plant material and stone, and the bodies of numerous beetles and larvae. The beetles were identified as a type of the carrion beetle, *Dermestes*, and their presence indicated that the body within had been seriously attacked by insects before the embalming and wrapping had been completed. Significantly, the outer wrappings had not been damaged by insects, and no insect remains were found in the first layers of cloth to be removed. The inner wrappings contained large quantities of beetles and larval skins, and extensive damage to both textiles and body came to light. It is clear that the beetles had hatched inside the

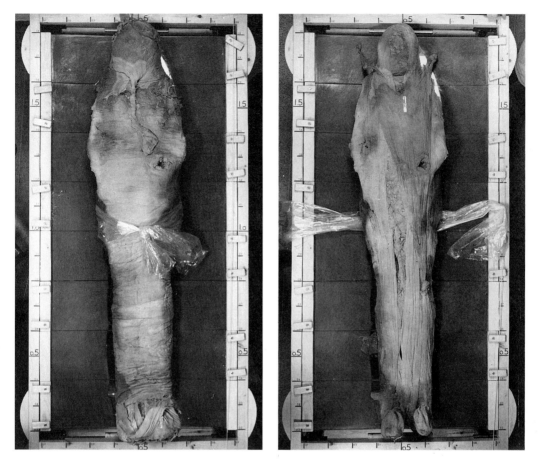

47 *(Above) A layer of narrow bandages wrapped around the body. Note the 'Osirian' beard imitated in twisted cloth.*

48 *(Above right) Granular packing material visible on the front of the body after the unwinding of the narrow strips of bandage.*

wrappings from eggs previously laid on the body, had devoured parts of the corpse, and died without reaching the surface of the wrappings. Several were disclosed inside the holes they had made as they tried to eat their way out.

After the removal of the outer wrappings the shape of the body of Horemkenesi was revealed enveloped in a shroud made from a long sheet torn in two and doubled in length by tying the two ends together. The putting on of this shroud seems to have marked the end of the application of the inner wrappings, and it was clear that care had been taken to ensure that the body was of the correct shape and had a firm surface, before the final stages of wrapping had begun. The measures taken by the embalmers to create the form they desired became apparent when removal of the shroud revealed masses of chalky white mud and scraps of cloth packed on and between the legs. The inner wrappings consisted of bandages wound individually around the limbs. The legs were tied together at the knees and ankles, and the hands held in position over the groin with a very tight twisted bandage.

Most of the inner layer of bandaging was heavily impregnated with

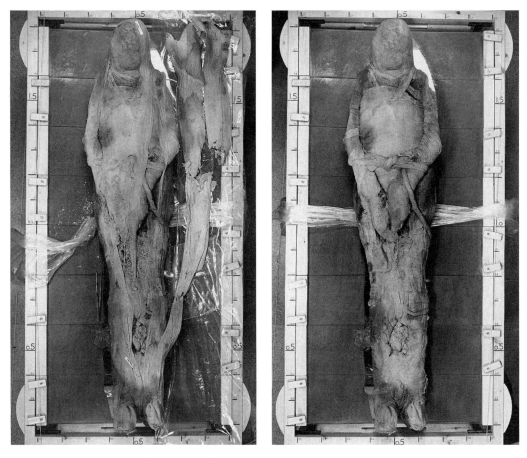

resin and adhered firmly to the skin, so that the layers had to be carefully prised apart using a scalpel. The application of large quantities of resin, a common feature of ancient Egyptian embalming procedure, frequently resulted in the wrappings becoming solidified into a hard mass. In several of the Twenty-first Dynasty mummies from the two Deir el-Bahri caches the outer and inner wrappings were separated by a thick 'carapace' of resinous paste. Extracting the body intact from such a hard layer has been a perennial problem for mummy-investigators. One public 'unrolling' by Pettigrew in 1837 had to be abandoned when it proved impossible to penetrate a thick coating of resin applied between layers of bandages, and as late as 1973, during the unwrapping of a mummy in the USA, a saw had to be used to cut simultaneously through layers of wrappings united into a dense mass by resin. In such situations it was hopeless to attempt to trace the original pattern of bandaging. The Bristol team were more fortunate, however, for although Horemkenesi's embalmers had applied large quantities of resin, this had not solidified the bandages inseparably, and in certain areas (notably the head) the wrappings had at some time been wet, causing the resin to dissolve. It

49 *(Above left) The first glimpse of the limbs, individually wrapped and bound tightly in place by thongs of twisted linen.*

50 *and* **51** *(Above and right) The arms and legs revealed. The position of the arms, extended over the front of the body, was typical for the Twenty-first Dynasty.*

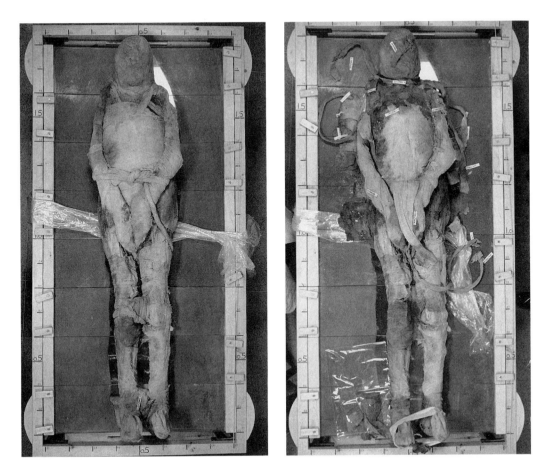

52 *(Above right) The inner wrappings in process of removal, each piece of cloth labelled and identified with a separate number.*

was possible, beginning at the head, to detach every fragment and to plot its position on drawings. Unexpected help came from the lights installed for the use of the camera crews, which diffused heat and softened the resin. Some dismembering had, with reluctance, to be done, however. The right arm was removed at the shoulder and the left detached at the elbow to give sufficient access to the sides of the body and to the arms themselves to enable them to be unwrapped.

When the last bandages were removed from the head, a large skull with shrunken facial features was revealed. The skin was brown in colour, leathery in texture, and saturated with resin. The eyes were still present, although they had lost their original shape and had sunk into the back of the orbits. The left eyebrow was well preserved. Most of the soft tissue of the nose had disintegrated but the interior bone structures were intact. Most of the right ear had disappeared but the left one was almost complete, including the pierced lobe. The mouth was wide open, revealing Horemkenesi's front teeth, yellow and loose in the sockets. The sides of the neck and parts of the face were riddled with holes made by the larvae of beetles which had devoured much of the skin and soft tissues. The head had been shaven (as a priest

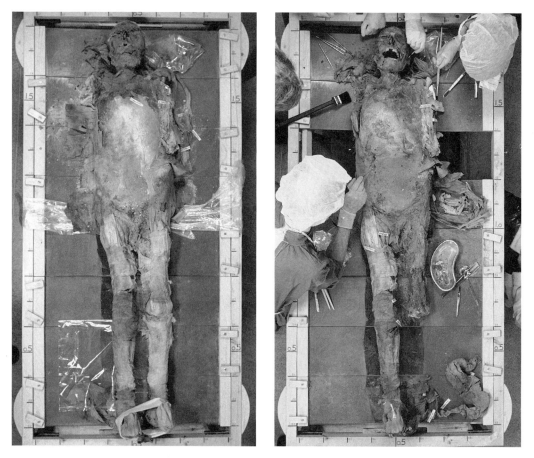

Horemkenesi would almost certainly have gone about his duties shaven-headed to ensure ritual purity), but short bristles could be seen, showing that the hairs on the scalp and eyebrows were black; the stubble of a black beard with some grey or white hairs was also visible.

The limbs and extremities were in poor condition. The muscle tissue in both arms was crumbling to powder, although the basic shape of the muscles could be discerned. The hands, which lay side by side over the pubic region, were in much better condition, and the skin of the fingers was sufficiently well preserved to permit members of the Avon and Somerset Police to obtain clear fingerprints – an exercise which, though performed on other mummies in recent years, never fails to stimulate the imagination; the fingerprints are one of the small details which poignantly emphasise the humanity of the subject and they helped to bridge the three-thousand-year gap separating the dead man from the modern world. The pubic region was entirely hidden by hard resinous material, and the genitals, though normally carefully preserved by the embalmers, were entirely missing. This is probably evidence for the poor condition of the body before mummification. The legs and feet, like the arms, were much

53 *(Above left) The head and torso of the mummy exposed. The arms have been removed to facilitate full recording.*

54 *(Above) Examination of the head and chest.*

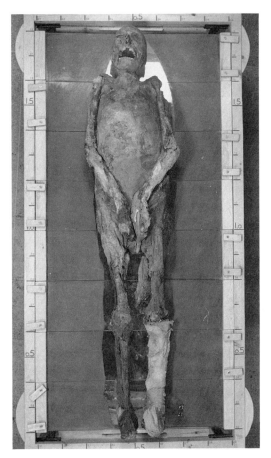

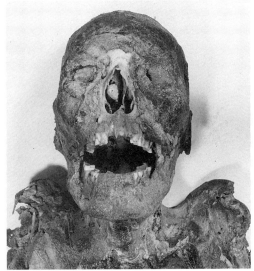

56 *(Below) Frontal view of the unwrapped head of Horemkenesi, showing the worn teeth and the loss of the soft tissue from the nasal area.*

55 *(Above) The mummy of Horemkenesi fully unwrapped and reassembled for photography, prior to dissection.*

damaged by insect activity; both legs became dislocated at the knees, revealing joints in good condition.

INTERNAL EXAMINATION: THE BODY CAVITY

An embalming incision, 13cm long, in the abdomen showed that Horemkenesi had been eviscerated in the standard way. The position of the cut was the typical one for the period – above and parallel to the left groin. There had been no attempt to close the incision by stitching, such as is known from at least two Twenty-first Dynasty mummies; it had simply been plugged with resin which had subsequently solidified. The heavy impregnation of the skin with resin had turned the surface of the chest and abdomen into a rigid, unyielding mass, and in order to conduct an internal examination the major portion of the chest and abdominal walls were cut away using an electric saw. The exposed body cavities were seen to be filled with very fine particles of mud, mixed with mineral fragments, seeds, straw and pieces of bandages – an alternative to the sawdust or powdered wood used to pack the body cavities of the majority of Twenty-first Dynasty mummies.

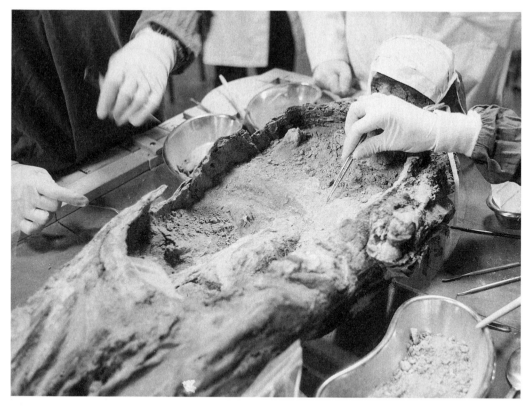

All the internal organs had been removed. Only the severed ends of the trachea and oesophagus remained; they had been cut through with a sharp tool, probably during the extraction of the viscera. The heart was also missing. This was highly unusual since the heart was believed to be the location of the intelligence, and it was expected that it would be weighed in the 'Balance of Judgement' before Osiris to determine whether or not its owner deserved to enter the afterlife. This episode was frequently depicted on the walls of the tombs, on coffins and on funerary papyri. Because of the importance of the heart, care was usually taken to leave it in position, and its absence in Horemkenesi's mummy was another clue to the condition of the body when the embalmers began their task. Although the material which had filled the cavity was carefully scrutinised by the investigators, not the slightest trace of any of the internal organs was found. A package which had shown up in the original X-ray examination of the mummy was, however, recovered. Although it measured only 15 × 10cm, hopes were raised that it might contain some of the missing organs. Disappointingly, it turned out to be simply a roll of linen, presumably inserted as packing.

When the last of the loose filling had been removed, with the aid of spoons, fine brushes and a vacuum cleaner, the interior of Horemkenesi's body could be examined in detail. The diaphragm

57 *Removal of the contents of the chest cavity, a mixture of mud, straw, seeds and scraps of linen.*

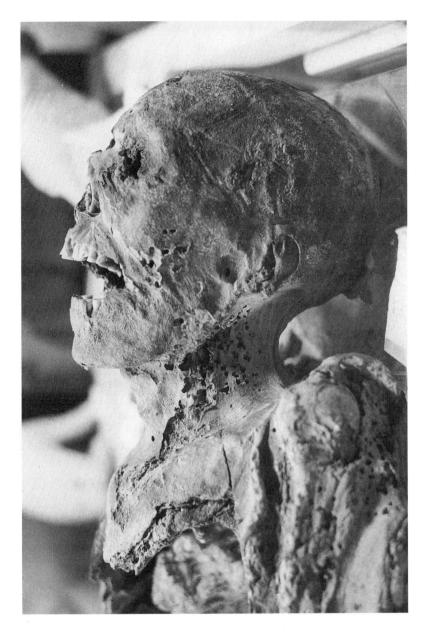

58 *The left side of the head. Insect damage to the face and neck is clearly visible.*

which separated the thoracic and abdominal cavities had disappeared, and small portions of large blood vessels and possible scar tissue were all that remained to indicate where the aorta and lungs had been removed by the embalmers. The lower pelvic area could not be examined in detail because of the presence of a concrete-like filling material which defeated attempts to dissect it.

THE HEAD

One of the most surprising findings was that Horemkenesi's brain

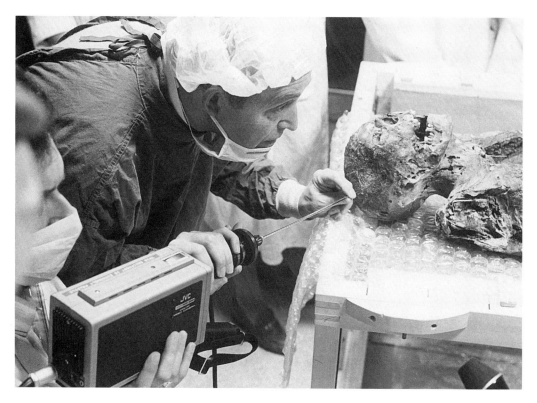

had not been removed by the embalmers. There was no evidence of the damage to the delicate nasal bones which normally resulted from the insertion of a metal hook into the nostril to gain access to the skull cavity; nor had the skull been perforated at any other point. Examination of the interior of the skull by Professor J. P. Mitchell, using an endoscope, revealed that the *dura mater*, the membrane which surrounds the brain, was largely intact, yet the brain itself had entirely disappeared. It is quite clear from Elliot Smith's studies of the mummies of the priests of Amun that removal of the brain was usual at this period, although instances are known where this was not done. The body of a young weaver called Nakht, who died during the Twentieth Dynasty and, like Horemkenesi, was buried at the temple of Mentuhotep II, was found on examination to retain the brain intact, but in this case mummification had not been performed at all; the body, with its internal organs in place, had simply been washed and wrapped, presumably to reduce expense. Horemkenesi, however, had certainly been properly embalmed according to the practices of his time – his body had been eviscerated and treated with natron – but as the examination proceeded the team uncovered evidence to suggest that the corpse had been already in a state of partial decomposition before the embalmers began work. This, together with the presence of beetle remains inside the skull (revealed

59 Examination of the interior of the skull using an endoscope inserted via a hole bored in one of the parietal bones. This confirmed the impression gained from X-rays that the brain was entirely absent.

by the endoscope), strongly suggested that the brain had been destroyed by natural decomposition and the activities of insects.

Thanks to the position of the widely gaping jaws, the well-preserved teeth could be scrutinised easily, though only fragments of the tongue survived. Insertion of an endoscope into the mouth and the thorax, made it possible to examine the upper part of the trachea and the larynx, revealing its internal structure and showing that the vocal cords were intact.

OTHER STUDIES

Examination of Horemkenesi's teeth yielded interesting results (pp. 100–1), and a series of studies was made on other parts of the body. The techniques of microbiology were applied to samples of soft tissue in an attempt to detect evidence of disease but no pathogenic organisms were identified. Examination of parts of the tongue by transmission electron microscopy, which permits greater magnification of tissue than ordinary light microscopy, revealed bacterial spores of the genus *Clostridia* in the tissue, though the exact species could not be identified. Some species of *Clostridia* cause diseases such as tetanus and botulism, but many others, much more common, occupy the intestines without any harmful effect, and it is most likely that the examples found in Horemkenesi's body owe their presence to contamination by bowel contents during the evisceration process in the embalmers' workshop.

60 *(Below left) Highly magnified view of* Clostridium *spores on the tongue.*

61 *(Below right) Shaved hair follicles on the face, revealed by scanning electron microscope.*

An important scientific tool for the study of disease in ancient bodies is histology and, in order to apply this to Horemkenesi, tissue samples were rehydrated by soaking them in a solution containing alcohol, sodium carbonate and formaldehyde. This is a standard procedure for softening mummified samples sufficiently to enable them to be cut into thin slices for microscopic examination. The sections were artificially stained, to reveal the structures of the tissues more clearly, and viewed under a microscope. This revealed the well-preserved structure of articular cartilage in one of the finger joints,

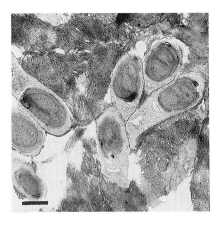

and elastic tissue in the skin and the walls of blood vessels, but no indication of disease was found, perhaps not surprisingly – the missing internal organs would have provided a far more promising basis for histological studies. Attempts to establish Horemkenesi's blood-group and tissue type proved unsuccessful, owing mainly to the large amount of resin with which the body had been impregnated.

The relatively poor state of preservation of the body was a disappointment, since this considerably reduced the amount of information that could be recovered about Horemkenesi's health. The most unfortunate aspect, however, was the absence of the internal organs, since these are potentially the most valuable source of information on diseases from which the individual might have suffered, and can also yield clues to the cause of death. However, this is not the end of the story. After the 1981 unwrapping, a large number of samples of hard and soft tissue from the body were reserved for future research and placed in storage; in 1994 samples were released for new research, and the results of this work (outlined in Chapter 6) have thrown new light on Horemkenesi's state of health. There is, then, good reason to suppose that the amount of data contained within his remains is far from being exhausted. Scientific techniques for identifying evidence of disease in mummified bodies are constantly being improved and at such time as new methods are applied, Horemkenesi will almost certainly tell us more about his life, and perhaps about his death.

CHAPTER SIX

The Embalming of
Horemkenesi

C ombining the evidence brought to light during the unwrapping with what is known about mummification from other
sources, it is possible to reconstruct the procedure followed
by the men who embalmed Horemkenesi.

Some form of taboo seems to have existed against the depiction in
funerary art of the embalming process, for representations of any part
of it are extremely rare. It is known that the place of embalming was
called the *wabet* ('pure place') or *per-nefer* ('house of rejuvenation'),
and attached to it or within it was a 'washing tent' (*ibu*), but little is
known of the nature or location of these workshops. It is likely that
they were lightly built structures, and that they were erected on the
west bank, close to the Nile since much water was required for the
washing of the corpse. Some evidence that the mummifying of
Horemkenesi took place near the river (or at least close to the
cultivation bordering the Nile) came to light during the unwrapping;
adhering to his shrouds and bandages were numerous small plant
fragments which turned out on study to include leaves of the *Tamarix
articulata*, grass *(Panicum repens L.* and *Lasiurus hirsutus*) and *Sorghum
vulgare*. Some of this material was probably windblown debris, picked
up from the floor of the embalmers' workshop during the preparation
of the wrappings. Its presence there suggests that the workshop stood
close to fields and water, and that it was well ventilated. Pollen
remains, which might have indicated at what time of year
Horemkenesi was mummified, were unfortunately not identified.

The most important stages of the mummification were carried out
with the body laid on a special table; the traditional type seems to
have had two sides carved in the shape of lions. A painting on the foot
of Horemkenesi's coffin shows the mummy, fully wrapped, lying

on such a table at the conclusion of the embalming process, with the gods Horus and Anubis in attendance. Miniature examples of these tables were discovered in the underground apartments of the pyramid complex of King Djoser at Saqqara, and full-sized ones for mummifying Apis bulls have been found at Memphis. These were made of calcite, but wooden embalming tables have also been found, some of which were much simpler; one found at Thebes, dating from the Middle Kingdom, comprised a flat baseboard with a series of supporting battens to enable the embalmers to gain access to the front and back of the corpse. The distinctive tools used in embalming are well known, thanks to the discovery of several examples in tombs, and even inside mummies, where they had been left by forgetful embalmers. They comprised a series of rods, hooks, spatulae, knives and tweezers, of copper or bronze. An important group of embalming implements found in the tomb of Ankh-hor at Thebes in 1982 also included a spouted cup rather like an enema, which was probably used to introduce liquids into the body.

The circumstances in which an ancient Egyptian died influenced the way his embalming was carried out. In a hot climate like that of Egypt, decomposition sets in immediately after death, affecting the internal organs first. Any delay in beginning the embalming process would make it more difficult to preserve the delicate internal parts. Horemkenesi had probably lain dead for some time – perhaps a few days (see p. 102) – before his body was found and brought to the embalmers' workshop, with results that would have been readily apparent. The brain was virtually destroyed and the viscera were probably in an advanced state of decay. Corruption may also have spread to the flesh, and it would have been necessary to work quickly in order to keep this under control.

Once Horemkenesi's clothing had been removed and the body had been washed, the embalmer had to consider whether or not to perforate the skull to extract what remained of the brain. As has been pointed out, endoscopy by the unwrapping team revealed that the surrounding membrane was substantially intact but that the brain itself had been eaten by the larvae of the carrion beetle, whose remains could be seen lying in the base of the skull. The embalmer's experience of bodies in different stages of decomposition probably convinced him that, in this case, he would be wasting his time; he therefore made no attempt to break the ethmoid bone or to make any other perforation in the skull.

Next, an incision was made in the left abdomen, above the groin. Through this all the internal organs were removed, including even the heart. Since the Old Kingdom it had been customary for the embalmers to preserve the liver, lungs, stomach and intestines using natron, to wrap them in linen and deposit them in a box or in four canopic jars which would be placed in the tomb. In Horemkenesi's time this custom had largely been superseded by the practice of replacing the four visceral packages inside the body cavity before the mummy was wrapped. A wooden canopic chest containing viscera, found in Horemkenesi's tomb, almost certainly belonged to Sadeh, the original occupant of the sepulchre, so it is fairly certain that Horemkenesi was buried without his inner organs. Their disappearance, and particularly the unusual absence of the heart, again point to the body's having been already in an advanced state of decomposition before mummification began. The embalmer was probably unable to preserve any of the organs, and confined himself to cleaning out the thoracic and abdominal cavities.

The next stage was to dry the body thoroughly, in order to eliminate all traces of moisture. The body cavities would have been filled with natron, which would also have been packed tightly around the corpse. It was left to dry, probably with other corpses in a special drying room, each identified by a label, until the allotted time – probably about forty days – had elapsed. By the end of this period the natron would have absorbed all the moisture from the body tissues. The embalmers uncovered the corpse and removed the natron from the cavity. In some instances, used or leftover natron was put into bags and buried in or near the tomb. As it had been in contact with the body and had absorbed the bodily fluids, it contained in a sense some part of the dead person and hence deserved burial, both to maintain the integrity of the body and to protect against any portion of it falling into the hands of enemies who might, through magic, be able to use it to harm the deceased.

The body was probably now washed once more, to remove all traces of the natron. This cannot have been done very thoroughly in Horemkenesi's case, however, for his wrappings became bleached and damaged through the effects of the natron, which turned some of the fibres to powder. Next, the cavities were packed. In other mummies of the Twenty-first Dynasty the skull cavity was filled with linen, introduced through the nose, but since Horemkenesi's skull had not been opened this was not done. The thoracic and abdominal cavities, however, were packed tightly with mud, inserted via the flank incision.

Although careful observations were made by the investigators, there was no indication that subcutaneous packing materials had been used in the preparation of Horemkenesi's mummy. No incisions were detected (with the exception of the abdominal incision made to extract the viscera) and no traces of packing materials were found underneath the skin. The omission of this treatment may be an indication that Horemkenesi was embalmed inexpensively, and that subcutaneous packing was deemed to be a luxury that could be dispensed with. But it is equally likely that the process had simply not yet been widely adopted at the time of Horemkenesi's death. Such packing is not found in the body of Nesamun, now in the Leeds Museum, who was embalmed at Thebes in the reign of Ramesses XI (c.1098–1069 BC) and it is only with the mummy of Nodjmet, wife of Herihor (probably a contemporary of Horemkenesi), that the first steps towards the practice can be observed. In Nodjmet's case, packing materials were applied to the external surface of the body; the earliest attempts at genuine subcutaneous packing so far identified (in the mummies of Henuttawy and the High Priest Masaharta, wife and son, respectively, of Pinedjem I, c.1070–1032 BC, or slightly later) were not completely successful because the embalmers overestimated the quantity of packing that would be needed, causing gross distortion of the facial features (fig. 31).

Other standard 'cosmetic' work, carried out before wrapping the body at this period, seems also to have been omitted in Horemkenesi's case: he was not provided with artificial eyes, his mouth was not closed, and no red ochre was applied to the skin. Neither was an incision plate placed over the embalming wound, but this was a frequent omission in the Twenty-first Dynasty mummies examined by Elliot Smith.

A large amount of resin was applied. As has been noted, this was a standard feature of Twenty-first Dynasty embalming practice. Besides excluding moisture and helping to give the corpse a pleasant odour, the resin probably aided preservation by antibiotic means. Scientific tests carried out on the embalming materials from Horemkenesi showed that there was present a constituent which inhibited the growth of bacteria. In all probability, this agent was the resin. Analysis of portions of skin from the body indicated that the resin which coated it was extracted from tree resins and plant waxes, though a specific identification was not achieved.

The corpse was now ready to be wrapped. The amount of time and attention devoted to the wrapping varied, probably according to cost. If the body were that of an important personage whose family possessed wealth and influence, the wrapping could take many days, to the accompaniment of incantations and the placing of amulets within the wrappings at specified locations relative to their function. These were designed for the protection of the deceased, and to promote his rebirth. In Horemkenesi's case the job was probably done quickly, using a miscellaneous array of cloth, and no amulets were provided at all.

The cloth which the embalmers now took up was the common undyed linen made from flax, in universal use throughout Egypt for clothes, sheets and other household articles. The presence of holes and repairs in several pieces shows that they were not new. Some had very likely formed parts of garments or pieces of bed linen (a variety of sheets, shirts, robes and other items including the sail of a boat have been found among the wrappings of mummies) but in no case could the original use of a piece be precisely determined. It is unknown where embalmers got their supplies of cloth for wrapping mummies. In Horemkenesi's case it is possible that at least some of the cloth had originally been made for his own domestic use; the two examples of his name written in black ink, found among the wrappings, are typical of the 'owner's marks', commonly written on everyday items such as clothes and sheets. Other pieces, however, may have come from temple or commercial workshops. Gillian Eastwood, who carried out the original study of Horemkenesi's wrappings, noted that one piece has a 'weaver's mark', a kind of 'signature' woven into the cloth. Such marks served to identify a particular workshop or weaver, and tended to be used by those working in weaving shops attached to temples. A distinctive arrangement of threads close to this mark may be equally diagnostic. The discovery of a similar arrangement on five other pieces of Horemkenesi's wrappings probably indicates that they had all been made by the same craftsman or in the same workshop. All told, however, the cloth used to wrap his body probably represents the work of several different workshops. Clues to this are indications that two different types of loom were used to make the cloth, and the variety of methods used to produce the fringes found on different pieces of the wrappings. If some of Horemkenesi's mummy-cloth came from temple workshops, this may be evidence that embalmers were supplied directly by such establishments; on the other hand, as a priest (even though of low rank) Horemkenesi may have had access to temple linen and so provided the cloth himself, along with old clothes and discarded bed covers.

In order to render this cloth suitable for wrapping a mummy, the embalmers tore some of the sheets into narrow strips. Larger pieces were also used as pads to help create the desired shape. The longest piece of cloth found was almost five metres in length. The careful recording of the unwrapping made it possible to make a tentative reconstruction of the sequence of wrapping, with drawings of every stage in the process.

The embalmers began by swathing the extremities separately. The wrapping of the head seems to have been done first. A pad of cloth was placed over the face and neck, and a bandage wrapped around them six times. A large bandage placed underneath the back was also twisted around the head, which was enveloped in a further six loops. Three bandages were wrapped around the neck to fill the space between the head and shoulders.

As a preliminary to wrapping the rest of the body, the embalmers laid two wide fringed bandages beneath the legs, drew them up the back and around the head, finally winding the ends around the arms. The order in which the torso, arms and legs were wrapped could not be definitely determined, but the method of wrapping each section is

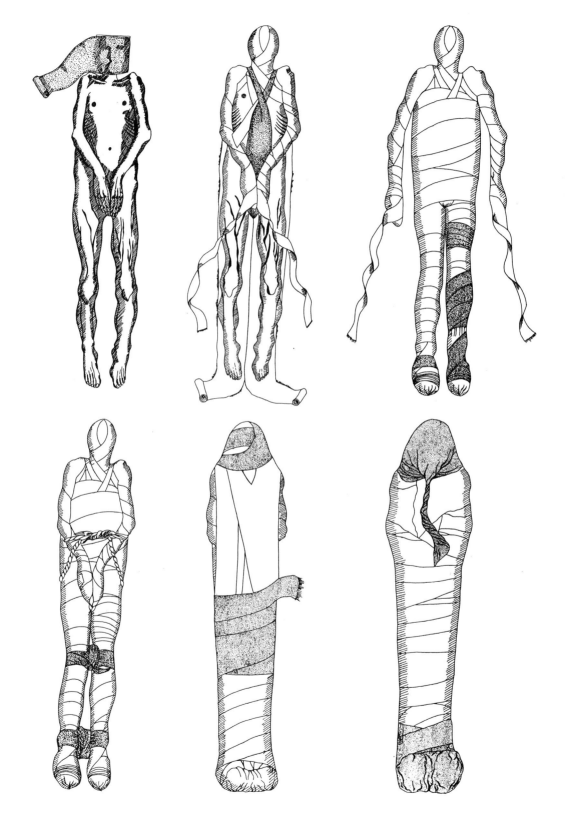

62 *Stages in the wrapping of Horemkenesi. A full series of drawings was made, recording the position of every piece of cloth and the order in which they had been applied.*

clear. The torso was covered with a sheet running from the left abdomen, around the neck to the right abdomen. Another two bandages were wound around the neck, and a sheet covering the front of the body was split so as to pass it around the neck. Another bandage was then wound around the body six times.

The legs and arms were then wrapped separately in long bandages, and were held together by means of tight bindings made of twisted strips. The wrapping proceeded with layers of narrow strips alternating with large sheets. Once the outer shroud was in place and had been firmly sealed with resin, the outer binding strips were arranged in the pattern customary at the time, and Horemkenesi's mummy was complete.

Study of the textiles revealed no clear pattern in the way the embalmers had used the different types of cloth they had at their disposal; the six similar pieces mentioned above, which evidently came from the same source, were used at various stages in the wrapping and placed on different parts of the body, from the neck to the heels. There was, however, some attempt to conceal the most worn and ragged portions of cloth by folding them so as to leave the best preserved areas visible.

Despite the time spent by the embalmers in eviscerating Horemkenesi, drying his body with natron and applying a resinous coating, their efforts were largely frustrated by *Dermestes frischii* and *Dermestes ater*, two varieties of the carrion beetle. As already mentioned, adult beetles had probably laid their eggs in the body before it was taken to be embalmed (or possibly while it was in the embalming workshop). After the wrapping was completed the beetle larvae, hatching from their eggs, began to devour the body, causing extensive damage, particularly to the neck, arms, legs and feet. Further traces of their activities were found on the legs, where microscopic examination revealed a mass of the faeces and cast-off skins of the larvae. Adult beetles had also eaten their way through the resinous coating protecting the skin and crept into the wrappings where some of them, unable to escape, eventually died; others probably mated and returned to the body to lay a new batch of eggs which, in due course, hatched to continue the infestation. *Dermestes* completes its life-cycle from egg to adult beetle in five weeks. Beetles preserve remarkably well, and many were found trapped within Horemkenesi's wrappings; a large group near the neck comprised 49 examples. In view of the serious nature of the infestation and the fact that the larvae can survive without water it is perhaps surprising that large sections of the flesh were unaffected by their activity; what finally arrested the destruction cannot be determined.

In Egypt's climate, carnivorous beetles and other insects would have attacked dead bodies very quickly unless precautions were taken to exclude them, and they were doubtless present in many

embalming workshops; the face of Tayuheret, a relative of the Theban High Priests of the Twenty-first Dynasty whose mummy was found in the Royal Cache at Deir el-Bahri, showed extensive insect damage similar to that on Horemkenesi's body. It is not surprising, then, that actual insect remains have often been found in mummies. *Dermestes* beetles were found in the skulls of several mummies examined in the early nineteenth century; Pettigrew mentions that one skull contained over 270 well-preserved adult specimens, together with remains of many others, suggesting that 'probably double that number lived, propagated their species, and died without ever seeing the light' (Pettigrew, 1834, 54–5, n.). The remains of flies and their puparia are also common finds within mummy wrappings, although none were identified in Horemkenesi. Since they would almost certainly have been originally present on his body, it is probable that they had simply laid their eggs, developed into adult flies and left the body before *Dermestes* began work; any fly larvae remaining would have been quickly consumed by those of the beetles.

63 *Samples of beetles recovered from the wrappings.*

CHAPTER SEVEN

The Findings: Reconstructing Horemkenesi the Man

PHYSICAL CHARACTERISTICS

Study of Horemkenesi's body enables us to visualise him in his later years as a short, rather plump man, clean-shaven and bald-headed, with a disfigured nose that gave him trouble in breathing. His stature in life, calculated from the lengths of the left femur and humerus, was about 168cm, though by the time he died he may have stooped due to osteoarthritis of the spine. Folds of skin observed in the lumbar region of his mummy indicate that he may have been somewhat obese.

In stature, build and shape of head Horemkenesi conforms to standard physical patterns for ancient Egyptians, as suggested by comparative studies of other skeletal material. His rather large head was meso-dolichocephalic (i.e. having a medium to long cranium), with a backwards-sloping forehead. It is usual for the human face to be slightly asymmetrical, and Horemkenesi's was no exception to this, but long before he died his appearance had been rendered more irregular still. Examination of the skull showed that he had once suffered a heavy blow to the face, which fractured and displaced the left nasal bone. The damage was not properly corrected, and as the visible traces of new bone growth show, the fracture healed with the nose twisted slightly to the right. The resulting constriction of the left nostril may have caused Horemkenesi permanent difficulty in breathing. One can only speculate as to how this happened – an accident? Or did an irate colleague punch him on the nose?

Greatly magnified images of the surface of the facial skin were obtained by means of scanning electron microscopy, revealing the tips of the beard stubble, which had clearly been cut by a sharp implement, indicating that Horemkenesi's face had been shaved shortly before or soon after death. A fissure was observed in the left ear-lobe (the corresponding section of the right ear had decomposed), possibly an indication that Horemkenesi's ears had been pierced for earrings. Perforations have been found in the ears of other priests' mummies of the Twenty-first Dynasty.

PATHOLOGICAL CONDITIONS

The ancient Egyptians were prey to many ailments arising from their environment, as well as to infectious diseases. Evidence for this comes from artistic representations and medical texts such as the Edwin Smith Papyrus and the Ebers Papyrus, recording the treatments recommended for various complaints, and also from the modern scientific study of mummies. Radiography and dissection of Horemkenesi's body by the original team of investigators revealed a number of pathological conditions, chiefly those associated with the ageing process. Mild degenerative spondylosis was demonstrated in the cervical and lumbar spine, together with narrowing of the spaces between all the joints in the hands and feet, and minor features of osteoarthritis in the shoulder joint. Such ailments are commonly found in Egyptian mummies, a high proportion of which exhibit arthritic changes, particularly in the spine. Horemkenesi was more fortunate than many of his compatriots, for his articular cartilages were free from calcification, a common condition which could effectively cripple the sufferer. More interesting from a medical viewpoint was the fusion of some of Horemkenesi's thoracic vertebrae, producing an appearance resembling 'dripping wax', a kind of ankylosis now known as Diffuse Idiopathic Skeletal Hyperostosis (DISH). This is very rare in young people, and today is present in only about five per cent of people over sixty. Sometimes associated with obesity, DISH does not have obvious symptoms, and in his case Horemkenesi may have been aware only of slight stiffness. None of these complaints would have caused serious disability, the symptoms amounting to little more than discomfort in the back, shoulders and neck – probably enough to make him irritable, but not to prevent him from living a normal life.

PARASITIC DISEASES

The Nile, whose waters and fertile silt provided the basis of life in ancient Egypt, was also a major source of ill health. Wet soils and stagnant waterways served as an excellent environment for various types of parasitic worm, which were a cause of widespread disease.

One of the commonest such ailments is schistosomiasis, which is endemic in modern Egypt, and has been detected in several mummies. It is caused by the bilharzia fluke, *Schistosoma haematobium*, which attaches itself to the walls of human blood vessels, and discharges eggs into the bloodstream. The eggs enter the host's bladder or intestine, and thence pass out of the body. If the eggs enter fresh water they hatch into larvae. These larvae enter the bodies of certain kinds of water snails, which act as an intermediate host. After developing further, the larvae move back to a human host, penetrating the skin and entering the blood vessels. Here they become mature bilharzia worms and attach themselves to the host's blood vessels again, where they lay eggs, and the life-cycle is repeated. Those whose occupations involved wading in water – herdsmen, fishermen, laundrymen – would have been particularly prone to the disease, but more casual contact with infested water (such as the occasional hunting or fowling trip in the marshes, or getting one's feet wet while crossing the river) could also have caused infection. There can be no doubt that schistosomiasis was widespread in ancient Egypt. The Ebers Papyrus describes various cures for blood in the urine, one of the classic symptoms of the complaint. The condition has also been diagnosed in mummies by the finding of calcified eggs of the worm in the preserved kidneys and liver, and by the radiological detection of calcification of the bladder, a method used successfully by the Manchester team.

In Horemkenesi's case it seemed at first unlikely that any evidence for the presence of parasitic disease could be recovered because of the absence of the internal organs. In 1990, however, an important non-destructive technique for identifying *Schistosoma* infection was announced by Robert Miller and co-workers. It depends on the detection, in preserved tissue, of the specific antigen produced during the infection by the continually regurgitated gut-lining of the adult schistosome worm. This antigen enters the bloodstream and is circulated to all living tissue in the host, where it can be detected. This method has been used successfully to demonstrate the presence of the disease in a corpse of late predynastic date in the British Museum – the earliest case of schistosomiasis so far known. Fortunately, the technique does not require the survival of the viscera, so it was possible for Miller to obtain results from a sample of Horemkenesi's skin – and this revealed the presence of schistosome circulating anodic antigen. This finding indicated not only that Horemkenesi had suffered from schistosomiasis, but that the disease was still active at the time he died, since the antigen disappears rapidly when the parasites are destroyed.

Given the relatively substantial evidence for schistosomiasis in ancient Egypt, it is not surprising to find that Horemkenesi had suffered from it. An altogether more remarkable discovery claimed by Robert Miller and his team was that Horemkenesi had suffered from malaria. Until very recently, the existence of malaria among the populations of ancient Egypt could only be deduced indirectly from scattered and ambiguous textual references. Now, however, immunological tests on mummified tissue have demonstrated the presence of malaria antigen in specimens ranging in date from the late predynastic period to the Late Period. When applied to a tissue sample from Horemkenesi, this test produced a positive result, indicating that he was suffering from untreated malaria at the time he died. The disease is carried by the mosquito, probably as prevalent in ancient Egypt as it is today.

TEETH

Horemkenesi's bodily aches and pains were probably negligible when compared with the discomfort he must have suffered from his teeth. Bread, which was the staple food of the ancient Egyptians, contained a high proportion of windblown sand, and this coarse material wore down the cusps of the teeth very quickly. The attrition of the teeth follows so regular a pattern that the degree of wear measurable on the three successive molars is often a reliable guide to the age of the subject at death. All of Horemkenesi's teeth were heavily worn, indicating that he was probably past middle age when he died (see below). Three teeth had been lost during life, including the first molars on each side. It is fairly certain that these losses were caused by abscesses at the roots of the teeth. Evidence for this is the serious damage to the adjacent alveolar bone, undoubtedly caused by the toxins from the abscesses. It is impossible to tell whether the teeth ultimately fell out or whether they had been deliberately extracted.

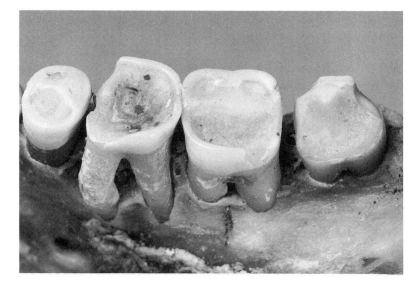

64 *Detail of Horemkenesi's lower left molar teeth, showing the effects of excessive wear.*

In response to continuous wear on the teeth a secondary layer of dentine is normally deposited to replace areas lost. Radiography of Horemkenesi's teeth, after unwrapping, showed that new dentine had indeed been formed where teeth had suffered serious wear. In cases where the pulp chamber (containing the tooth's blood supply) becomes exposed due to extreme wear on the teeth or failure to replace the dentine, bacteria are able to enter, and abscesses quickly form. The pulp chambers in two of Horemkenesi's teeth had become exposed and abscesses had developed here, as well as below the three teeth he had lost.

Horemkenesi's abscesses must have caused him much pain and discomfort. The infection from two of the molars in his upper jaw spread to the maxillary sinuses, and a patch of wrinkled skin on the right cheek may have marked the point where the pus from one of the abscesses had made its escape. It is still a matter for debate whether the ancient Egyptians attempted to relieve the pain of dental abscesses by surgery (for example, by drilling into the gum or bone to allow the pus to escape), but pharmaceutical methods of dealing with the problem certainly existed. The Ebers Papyrus contains two prescriptions for treating abscesses; one, made from cow's milk and earth almonds, was 'to be placed in the evening dew' before being used as a mouthwash; the other recipe called for cumin, terebinth (turpentine) and colocynth 'to be made into a powder and applied to the teeth'. These remedies may have reduced the degree of pain (terebinth possesses antiseptic qualities and was commonly used by ancient Egyptian physicians) but could not have provided permanent relief. Besides the serious damage caused by attrition, two of Horemkenesi's teeth exhibit cavities caused by caries. Caries is a condition highly characteristic of modern society, with its high-sugar diet. It does not seem to have been a common complaint among ancient Egyptians, since their diet was largely free from cariogenic substances. Honey, however, used by the Egyptians as a sweetener in cakes, can cause caries, and it is possible that this was responsible for the affected areas of Horemkenesi's teeth.

AGE AND CIRCUMSTANCES OF DEATH

In ancient bodies, the state of the teeth are the most reliable guide to the age at death, but this evidence is mainly of value in assessing relatively young people. The worn condition of Horemkenesi's teeth indicates that he was not a young man, but does not permit greater precision than this. The degree and situation of the degenerative spondylosis, and the DISH affecting Horemkenesi's spine are consistent with an age at death of fifty to sixty. While an 'average life expectancy' for ancient Egyptians is difficult to establish (in part owing to the difficulty of assessing ages at death from mummified remains), it is clear that many of those who were mummified (and who, therefore, were probably among the more affluent and better-nourished members of society) died before they were forty. Horemkenesi's death, then, would have been regarded as by no means premature.

Because of the absence of recent fractures to the bones or obvious damage to the soft tissues it is very unlikely that Horemkenesi's death resulted from physical trauma. Other possible causes, however, cannot be so easily eliminated: the loss of the internal organs deprives us of the chance to discover whether or not Horemkenesi had suffered from some fatal disease; nor can we rule out causes of death which leave only minor traces on a mummified body, such as drowning, suffocation or poisoning.

Although the exact cause of his death cannot be determined from the body, some attempt can be made to reconstruct the circumstances in which Horemkenesi may have died. As we have seen, the body was probably in poor condition before it was delivered to the embalmers, having become infested with insects and their larvae. Although the discovery of insects within mummies is not uncommon (p. 96), the infestation of Horemkenesi's body was particularly serious, perhaps suggesting that the interval between death and embalming was longer than usual. It was observed that the face and hands were generally better preserved than other parts of the body, a situation that might be accounted for if the body had been lying prone on a sandy surface with the hands beneath. Particularly significant in this respect was the good condition of the eyes. These would be quickly attacked by insects, and their preservation may well have resulted from the face having been in contact with the ground, preventing insects from gaining access to them.

A hypothesis which accounts for all the facts was postulated by Norman Brown, the pathologist who studied the remains. According to Brown's scenario, Horemkenesi may have suffered a stroke, heart attack or internal haemorrhage. Collapsing face down on the ground, he would have died after a short time. If this had happened in one of the remoter parts of the west bank his body might have lain undiscovered for hours or even days. When at last it was found it was, no doubt, taken to be mummified without delay. The embalmers, however, finding decomposition well advanced, were unable to preserve the entire corpse according to the traditional method; they did not attempt to perforate the skull, and simply disposed of what remained of the organs of the thorax and abdomen.

The Open Mouth

While it is not uncommon to find mummies with mouths slightly open, widely gaping mouths such as Horemkenesi's are unusual. The reason for this peculiarity is not known. Examination of the mandible showed that it had not been dislocated or fractured. It is possible that some muscular spasm occurring at the time of Horemkenesi's death fixed the jaws in this position and that the embalmers, working quickly, did not attempt to close the mouth. When an individual dies in a relaxed state the lips and teeth are normally parted slightly. But if death occurs at a moment of high excitement or fear, a spasm of the muscles in the face may cause the jaws to open widely and to remain in this state after death. It is possible then that some aspect of the circumstances surrounding Horemkenesi's death produced this state of affairs. In the absence of any sign of bodily injury which might suggest a violent death one can only speculate as to what this might have been. It is none the less strange that the mouth was not filled with packing materials, according to the usual custom of Horemkenesi's time.

RECONSTRUCTION OF THE FACE

When studying an ancient mummy it is not always easy to remember that the subject was once a living, breathing person, especially as the shrunken and distorted features of most mummified heads give only a very imperfect impression of the individual's appearance in life. To help visualise the living person, an aspect of several of the scientific mummy investigations of recent years has been the reconstruction of the faces of ancient Egyptian subjects, based on skulls. Fundamental background work in the field of facial reconstruction was done by J. Kollman and W. Büchly who in 1898 published details of the thickness of the soft tissues at 23 different points on the skull. These measurements formed the basis for the heads made for Manchester Museum, representing the 'Two Brothers', found in a Twelfth Dynasty tomb at Rifeh, and the unidentified young woman '1770'. Methods for building up the face from the skull have been used successfully in police work to identify badly decomposed bodies. Although an exact likeness is unlikely to be produced in this way, controlled experiments have shown that the resulting images are accurate enough to make recognition possible. Reconstructions made using the skulls of anatomy subjects, when afterwards compared with photographs of the actual faces taken before embalming, proved to be significantly similar.

Horemkenesi's skull was carefully preserved with a view to making a reconstruction of his face as it might have appeared in life. The head was detached from the body, and the remaining flesh removed. An initial obstacle to obtaining an accurate image of Horemkenesi in life was the open mouth, which first had to be closed by detaching and repositioning the mandible. When this was done it was found that the joints on which the jaw hinged were in no way damaged or deformed.

The reconstruction was made by the sculptor Ernest Pascoe. A three-piece mould was made from the skull, and three casts were produced from it using dental plaster. Small lengths of aluminium

rod were inserted into the cast of the skull, and left projecting at specific distances, each rod indicating the usual depth of soft tissue at a particular point on the human head and face. The missing tissue was imitated using clay, which was first applied around the aluminium rods and gradually extended outwards until the entire skull was covered. This process was tested on one of the three casts, reconstructing only the left half of the head. Then, using another cast of the skull, the process was repeated until the whole head was built up. In the later stages of the modelling, individual peculiarities such as Horemkenesi's crooked nose and blocked nostril were added. The

65 *Horemkenesi adoring the goddess Hathor, in the form of a cow standing on the slopes of the Theban necropolis; a painting on the side of his coffin.*

appearance of the nose could be deduced with some confidence from the way in which the bone had healed after it had been fractured. Superficial signs of age such as facial wrinkles, however, are either eliminated or greatly distorted by the embalming process, and their original appearance can only be conjectured. Horemkenesi's age at death was estimated at about fifty to sixty years, so it could be safely assumed that half a century's exposure to the Egyptian climate had left its mark on the surface of his face, and wrinkles were added accordingly.

The full head was cast and patinated to resemble a bronze sculpture. It was felt that the likeness thus created, though not naturalistically coloured, would be more accessible (in terms of the human response of museum visitors) than some other reconstructions of mummies, in which the artificial colouring of the skin and the inlaid eyes produce an unreal effect like that of a wax effigy. The half-head, however, was coloured for use as an instructional model.

The development of more advanced techniques means that in the future such reconstructions may be made from models of skulls created with the aid of a CT scanner, eliminating the need to unwrap and dissect the body. Non-destructive studies, indeed, are likely to be the basis of most future research on mummies. Increasingly sophisticated imaging methods such as CT scanning enable the scientist to visualise what lies beneath the bandages, to determine the subject's sex, age and state of health at death, and even to discover the shape and composition of amulets and other objects placed there by the embalmers. The rapid progress of study of ancient DNA promises to have even greater consequences for our understanding of the lives of the ancient Egyptians. With the steady improvement of these scientific techniques the amount of information which can be obtained non-invasively, or with only minimal disturbance to the remains, is increasing. Hence the unwrapping of a mummy has become a rare event, and will probably be still rarer in the future, as new methods for gathering evidence are developed.

Chronological Table

PREDYNASTIC PERIODS
*c.*4500–3000 BC

EARLY DYNASTIC
Dynasties 1–3
*c.*3100–2613 BC

OLD KINGDOM
Dynasties 4–8
*c.*2613–2160 BC

FIRST INTERMEDIATE PERIOD
Dynasties 9–10 and Dynasty 11 in southern Upper Egypt
*c.*2160–2025 BC

MIDDLE KINGDOM
Dynasties 11–13 over all Egypt
*c.*2025–1700 BC

SECOND INTERMEDIATE PERIOD
Dynasty 13 over Upper Egypt and Dynasties 14–17
*c.*1700–1550 BC

NEW KINGDOM
Dynasty 18
*c.*1550–1295 BC
Dynasty 19
*c.*1295–1186 BC
Dynasty 20
*c.*1186–1069 BC

THIRD INTERMEDIATE PERIOD
Dynasty 21
*c.*1069–945 BC
Dynasties 22–23
*c.*945–727 BC

LATE PERIOD
Dynasties 24–30 and Persian occupation
*c.*727–332 BC

PTOLEMAIC PERIOD
332–30 BC

ROMAN PERIOD
30 BC–AD 330

BYZANTINE PERIOD
AD 330–641

ISLAMIC PERIOD
After AD 641

Bibliography

ANDREWS, C., *Egyptian Mummies*. London, 1984.

ARNOLD, D., *Der Tempel des Königs Mentuhotep von Deir el-Bahari*. I-III. Mainz am Rhein, 1974 and 1981.

ARNOLD, D., *The Temple of Mentuhotep at Deir el-Bahari*. New York, 1979.

BIERBRIER, M. L., *The Late New Kingdom in Egypt (c.1300–664 BC)*. Warminster, 1975.

BIERBRIER, M. L., *The Tomb-builders of the Pharaohs*. London, 1982.

ČERNY, J., *Graffiti Hiéroglyphiques et Hiératiques de la Nécropole Thébaine (Documents de Fouilles de l'Institut Français d'Archéologie Orientale du Caire 9)*, Cairo, 1956, 20, 21, 22, pls. 58, 60 (graffiti 1313, 1322 and 1343).

ČERNY, J., 'Egyptian Oracles' in PARKER, R. A., *A Saite Oracle Papyrus from Thebes*. Providence, 1962, 35–48.

ČERNY, J., *A Community of Workmen at Thebes in the Ramesside Period*. Cairo, 1973.

ČERNY, J. and SADEK, A. A., *Graffiti de la Montagne Thébaine*, III. Cairo, 1970, pl. 76; IV. Cairo, 1970, 42 (graffito 2138).

COCKBURN, A. and E., *Mummies, Disease and Ancient Cultures*. Cambridge, 1980.

DAVID, R. (ed.), *The Manchester Museum Mummy Project*. Manchester, 1979.

DAVID, R. and TAPP, E. (eds), *Evidence Embalmed. Modern medicine and the mummies of ancient Egypt*. Manchester, 1984.

DAVID, R. and TAPP, E. (eds), *The Mummy's Tale. The scientific and medical investigation of Natsef-Amun, priest in the temple at Karnak*. London, 1992.

DEELDER, A. M., MILLER, R. L., DE JONGE, N., and KRIJGER, F. W., 'Detection of schistosome antigen in mummies', *The Lancet*, 335 (24 March 1990), 724–5.

GALERIES NATIONALES DU GRAND PALAIS, *Tanis. L'Or des Pharaons*. Paris, 1987.

GERMER, R., *Mumien. Zeugen des Pharaonenreiches*. Zürich and Munich, 1991.

GOYON, J-C., *Rituels Funéraires de l'Ancienne Égypte*. Paris, 1972.

HELCK, W., 'Priester' in *Lexikon der Ägyptologie*, IV. Wiesbaden, 1982, 1084–97.

HÖLSCHER, U., *The Mortuary Temple of Ramses III*, I–II (*The Excavation of Medinet Habu*). Chicago, 1941, 1951.

HÖLSCHER, U., *Post-Ramessid Remains* (*The Excavation of Medinet Habu*). Chicago, 1954.

JANSEN-WINKELN, K., 'Das Ende des Neuen Reiches', *Zeitschrift für Ägyptische Sprache und Altertumskunde* 119 (1992), 22–37.

JANSEN-WINKELN, K., 'Der Beginn der Libyschen Herrschaft in Ägypten', *Biblische Notizen* 71 (1994), 78–97.

JANSEN-WINKLEN, K., 'Die Plünderung der Königsgräber des Neuen Reiches', *Zeitschrift für Ägyptische Sprache und Altertumskunde* 122 (1995), 62–78.

JANSSEN, J., J., *Commodity Prices from the Ramessid Period*. Leiden, 1975.

JANSSEN, R. M. and J. J., *Growing up in ancient Egypt*. London, 1990.

KEES, H., *Das Priestertum im Ägyptischen Staat vom Neuen Reich bis zur Spätzeit*. Leiden-Köln, 1953.

KEES, H., *Die Hohenpriester des Amun von Karnak von Herihor bis zum Ende der Äthiopenzeit*. Leiden, 1964.

KITCHEN, K., *The Third Intermediate Period in Egypt*. Warminster, 1972; *Supplement*, Warminster, 1986.

KRUCHTEN, J-M., *Le grande texte oraculaire de Djéhoutymose, Intendant du Domaine d'Amon sous le pontificat de Pinedjem II*. Brussels, 1986.

KRUCHTEN, J-M., *Les Annales des Pretres de Karnak (XXI-XXIIImes Dynasties) et autres textes contemporains relatifs à l'initiation des pretres d'Amon*. Leuven, 1989.

LEGRAIN, G., 'Le logement et transport des barques sacrées et des statues des dieux dans quelques temples Égyptiens', *Bulletin de l'Institut Français d'Archéologie Orientale* 13 (1917), 1–76, pls. I–VII.

LESKO, L. H. (ed.), *Pharaoh's Workers. The Villagers of Deir el Medina*. Ithaca and London, 1994.

MILLER, R. L., DE JONGE, N., KRIJGER, F. W. and DEELDER, A. M., 'Predynastic Schistosomiasis' in DAVIES, W. V. and WALKER, R. (eds), *Biological Anthropology and the Study of Ancient Egypt*. London, 1993, 54–60.

MILLER, R. L. et al., 'Diagnosis of *Plasmodium falciparum* infections in mummies using the rapid manual *ParaSight™-F* test', *Transactions of the Royal Society of Tropical Medicine and Hygiene* 88 (1994), 31–2.

NAGUIB, S-A., *Le Clergé Féminin d'Amon Thébain a la 21e Dynastie*. Leuven, 1990.

NAVILLE, E. and HALL, H. R., 'Excavations at Deir el-Bahari', *Egypt Exploration Fund Archaeological report 1904–5*, 1–10, pls. 1–4.

NAVILLE, E., HALL, H. R. and AYRTON, E. R., *The XIth Dynasty Temple at Deir el-Bahari*, I. London, 1907.

NIWINSKI, A., 'The Solar-Osirian unity as principle of the theology of the 'State of Amun' in Thebes in the 21st Dynasty', *Jaarbericht Ex Oriente Lux* 30 (1987–88), 89–106.

NIWINSKI, A., *21st Dynasty Coffins from Thebes. Chronological and Typological Studies*. Mainz am Rhein, 1988.

NIWINSKI, A., *Studies on the illustrated Theban funerary papyri of the 11th and 10th centuries BC*. Freiburg and Göttingen, 1989.

NIWINSKI, A., 'Bürgerkrieg, militärischer Staatsreich und Ausnahmezustand in Ägypten unter Ramses XI. Ein Versuch neuer Interpretation der alten Quellen' in GAMER-WALLERT, I. and HELCK, W. (eds), *Gegengabe. Festschrift für Emma Brunner-Traut*. Tübingen, 1992, 235–62.

O'CONNOR, D., 'New Kingdom and Third Intermediate Period, 1552–664 BC' in TRIGGER, B. G., KEMP, B. J., O'CONNOR, D. and LLOYD, A. B., *Ancient Egypt. A Social History*. Cambridge, 1983, 183–278.

ORIENTAL INSTITUTE, UNIVERSITY OF CHICAGO. *The Temple of Khonsu, I: Scenes of King Herihor in the Court*. Chicago, 1979.

PETTIGREW, T. J., *A History of Egyptian Mummies*. London, 1834.

SADEK, A. F., *Graffiti de la Montagne Thébaine*, III/4, Cairo, 1972, pl. CCIV; IV/3, Cairo, 1972, 160 (graffito 3123).

SAUNERON, S., *The Priests of Ancient Egypt*. London and New York, 1960.

SMITH, G. ELLIOT., 'A Contribution to the study of mummification in Egypt', *Mémoires présentés a l'Institut Égyptien* 5 (1906), 3–53, pls. I–XIX.

SMITH, G. ELLIOT., 'An account of the mummy of a priestess of Amen supposed to be Ta-usert-em-suten-pa', *Annales du Service des Antiquités de l'Égypte* 7 (1906), 155–82, pls. I–IX.

SPIEGELBERG, W., *Ägyptische und andere Graffiti (Inschriften und Zeichnungen) aus der Thebanischen Nekropolis*. Heidelberg, 1921, 85, Taf. 114 (graffito 1012).

VALBELLE, D., *'Les Ouvriers de la Tombe.' Deir el-Médineh à l'Époque Ramesside*. Cairo, 1985.

VOGELSANG-EASTWOOD, G., *Patterns for Ancient Egyptian Clothing*. Leiden, 1992.

WEEKS, K. R., 'Ancient Egyptian Dentistry' in HARRIS, J. E. and WENTE, E. F. (eds), *An X-Ray Atlas of the Royal Mummies*. Chicago and London, 1980, 99–121.

WENTE, E. F., *Late Ramesside Letters*. Chicago, 1967.

Illustration Acknowledgements

Abbreviations:
BCMAG By courtesy of Bristol City Museum and Art Gallery
BM By courtesy of the Trustees of the British Museum
EES Egypt Exploration Society, London
UCOI By courtesy of the Oriental Institute of the University of Chicago

Front cover: Martin R. Davies.
Frontispiece: BCMAG.

1   From H. Hall, 'Edward Ayrton', *Journal of Egyptian Archaeology* 2 (1915), pl. VI. Reproduced courtesy of EES.
2   From *Biblia* III/6 (Sept. 1890), 80.
3   BM.
4   From E. Naville and H. R. Hall, 'Excavations at Deir el-Bahari', *Egypt Exploration Fund Archaeological Report, 1904–5*, pl. I. Reproduced courtesy of EES.
5   Drawing by Claire Thorne.
6   BM.
7   BCMAG H 641.
8   Drawn by Claire Thorne after W. Spiegelberg, *Ägyptische und andere Graffiti (Inschriften und Zeichnungen) aus der Thebanischen Nekropolis*, Heidelberg, 1921, Taf. 114.
9   Drawing by Claire Thorne.
10   BM.
11   Graham Harrison.
12   John H. Taylor.
13   UCOI. From *The Temple of Khonsu, I. Scenes of King Herihor in the Court*, Chicago, 1979, pl. 32.
14   John H. Taylor.
15   BM.
16   Photography by the Egyptian Expedition, the Metropolitan Museum of Art, New York.
17   T. G. H. James.
18   BM.
19   Drawing by Claire Thorne.
20   From G. Maspero, 'Les Momies Royales de Deir el-Bahari', *Mémoires de la Mission Archéologique Française au Caire* 1 (1889), pl. XVII B.
21   BM.

22   UCOI. From U. Hölscher, *The Mortuary Temple of Ramses III*, I (*Excavations at Medinet Habu*), Chicago, 1941, pl. 13 B.
23   BM.
24   UCOI. From U. Hölscher, *The Mortuary Temple of Ramses III*, II (Excavations at Medinet Habu), Chicago, 1951, pl. 2 (drawing by Harald Hanson).
25   UCOI. From U. Hölscher, *Post-Ramessid Remains* (*Excavations at Medinet Habu*), Chicago, 1954, pl. 5 A.
26   From N. de Garis Davies and A. H. Gardiner, *Seven Private Tombs at Kurnah*, London, 1948, pl. XIII. Reproduced by courtesy of EES.
27–9 BCMAG H 641.
30   From G. Elliot Smith, *The Royal Mummies* (*Catalogue Géneral du Musée du Caire*), Cairo, 1912, pl. LXIX.
31   From E. Brugsch and G. Maspero, *La Trouvaille de Deir-el-Bahari*, Cairo, 1881: supplementary plate in copy formerly belonging to Major W. J. Myers, Eton College.
32   From G. Elliot Smith, 'A Contribution to the study of mummification in Egypt', *Mémoires présentés a l'Institut Égyptien* 5 (1906), pl. III.
33–5 BCMAG H 641.
36   BM.
37–42 BCMAG.
43   Jonathan Musgrave.
44–56 BCMAG.
57   Jonathan Musgrave.
58   Jonathan Musgrave.
59   Jonathan Musgrave.
60–61 The late Norman J. Brown.
62   David Dawson.
63   BCMAG.
64   Courtesy of the Natural History Museum, London.
65   BCMAG H641.

Colour illustrations:
I–IV: BCMAG H641.
V–VI: Roger Scruton/Sunday Times.
VII: Martin R. Davies.
VIII: BCMAG.

Index

Roman numerals in **bold** refer to colour illustrations. Arabic numerals in **bold** refer to pages with black and white illustrations.